Leo Butl
Plays: 2

D0985504

Airbag; I'll Be the Devil; Faces in the Crowd;
Juicy Fruits; 69; Do It!

I'll Be the Devil: 'A gripping play and an extraordinary piece of writing which comes at you in a blizzard of diseased banter.' *Daily Mail*

Faces in the Crowd: 'Butler's outstanding play is a raw and devastating account of a couple who got swept along on a tide of easy credit, only to end up dashed against a northern rock of debt. It is a timely, savage, brilliant theatrical epitaph for the New Labour decade of shattered hopes and dreams turned sour.' *Daily Telegraph*

Juicy Fruits: 'Butler is interested in the way women cope with the trauma of childbirth and the shock of infant death, showing us two characters trying to carry on as if their lives were unchanged by events that have left them lonely, manic and bereaved.' *Guardian*

69: 'Let's talk about sex: intelligently, humorously, candidly and brazenly . . . and we respond by devouring each intimate yet brief encounter' *Metro*

Leo Butler was born in Sheffield. His work includes *Made of Stone, Redundant, Lucky Dog, Faces in the Crowd* (Royal Court Theatre); *Devotion* (Theatre Centre); *Heroes* (National Theatre Education Tour); *I'll Be the Devil* (RSC/Tricycle Theatre); *The Early Bird* (Queen's Theatre, Belfast/Finborough Theatre); *Juicy Fruits* (Paines Plough/Traverse Theatre/Royal Exchange Theatre, Manchester); *69* (Pleasance Courtyard, Edinburgh Festival); *Could You Please Close the Door Please* (FIND Festival/Schaubühne, Berlin); *Alison! A Rock Opera* (co-composed with Daniel Persad, Royal Court Theatre/King's Head Theatre/Spread Eagle Theatre); and *Boy* (Almeida Theatre).

Leo Butler
Plays: 2

Airbag

I'll Be the Devil

Faces in the Crowd

Juicy Fruits

69

Do It!

with an introduction by the author

Bloomsbury Methuen Drama
An imprint of Bloomsbury Publishing Plc

B L O O M S B U R Y
LONDON • OXFORD • NEW YORK • NEW DELHI • SYDNEY

Bloomsbury Methuen Drama

An imprint of Bloomsbury Publishing Plc

50 Bedford Square	1385 Broadway
London	New York
WC1B 3DP	NY 10018
UK	USA

www.bloomsbury.com

Bloomsbury is a registered trade mark of Bloomsbury Publishing Plc

This collection first published 2016

I'll Be the Devil first published in 2008 by Methuen Drama
© Leo Butler 2008, 2016

Faces in the Crowd first published in 2008 by Methuen Drama
© Leo Butler 2008, 2016

Airbag, Juicy Fruits, 69 and *Do It!* first published in this collection 2016
© Leo Butler 2016

This collection copyright © Leo Butler 2016
Introduction copyright © Leo Butler 2016

British Library Cataloguing-in-Publication Data
A catalogue record for this book is available from the British Library.

ISBN: HB: 971-8-3500-0629-4
PB: 978-1-3500-0628-7
EPDF: 978-1-3500-0630-0
EPUB: 978-1-3500-0631-7

Cover image © Roberto Schmidt/Getty Images

Library of Congress Cataloging-in-Publication Data
A catalog record for this book is available from the Library of Congress.

Typeset by Country Setting, Kingsdown, Kent

Contents

Leo Butler
Select Chronology

Introduction

1

We were watching Femi Kuti rehearsing with his band in the Africa Shrine. It was towards the end of 2007. Ramin Gray and I were in Lagos, running playwriting workshops for the Royal Court and an evening out was a rare treat, not least to see some live music.

We'd had a few beers and we were talking about some of the bands we'd been to see over the years. Arthur Lee and Love at the Sheffield Leadmill in 2005 was definitely up there for me, but Ramin had seen Bob Marley and the Wailers at the Rainbow Theatre in 1977, and there was no way I could compete with that.

The Africa Shrine is a sprawling, dimly lit social club somewhere on the outskirts of the city, and it was packed with guys who'd come to watch a Manchester United game on the giant screens above the bar. English football's big business in Nigeria. There are Chelsea flags pinned to the backs of all the buses, and when I told the locals that I supported Sheffield United I was met with howls of laughter.

So it was evening and the British Council had driven us out to the Shrine in a bullet-proof van. They weren't taking any chances – we had an armed guard too.

We drove past a woman selling pots and pans at the side of the road. She was illuminated by flames bursting out from the top of an abandoned oil drum.

One of us, I can't remember who, pointed to her and said 'Maryanne'.

As we sat in the Shrine talking about Bob Marley, a man with no legs served us drinks. Perched on a wooden trolley, he scooted through the crowds, whizzed under and around the tables. After he'd finished taking our orders he surprised us again by jumping off the trolley, lifting it high above his head. He stacked up the empties, turned and hurdled back to the bar on one hand.

One of us, I can't remember who, pointed to him and said 'Pot-Boy'.

2

'Are you busy?'

'Oh. you know . . .'

'Well. remember how we did *The Early Bird* in the perspex box at the Finborough? We're kind of expanding that concept with this one. It's another box, but it's sealed off, covered up this time, like a peep show? The plays happen inside, it's sealed off and sound-proofed. and so the audience come in and they have their own little cubicle . . .'

'Just like a peep show.'

'Just like a peep show. yeah. but they have these headphones. We've got an amazing sound designer and they put on their head-phones and watch the play through a screen. a little sort of glass window. And we'll have two or three plays in rep, maybe a band some nights, a cabaret, burlesque or something – all very different, a really diverse set of writers I think. and each of the plays is going to be about sex, challenging . . . ideas about sex, sexuality, voyeur-ism. And. it's fine. you can do whatever you want, be explicit as you want, or. you know. not at all if you don't want.

'What if someone decides to have a wank?'

'In the cubicle. you mean? Well. I guess we'll cross that bridge when we come to it. The point is to subvert and surprise and . . . challenge or redefine the lines between the play and the audience. Why don't you go away and think about it?'

3

On 19 Oct 2011, at 00:31, leo butler wrote:

Dear ****,

Thank you for your review of *Juicy Fruits* the other day. I'm pleased that you saw some potential in the main character, and I apologise that some of the humour was in bad taste. I would welcome your thoughts on how I might improve the piece.

However, I feel I should point out that the final scene was not a production gimmick, but a scripted scene with dialogue and stage directions.

All best,

Leo.

10/19/11 at 9:46 AM
To: leo butler
Hi. Leo,
    Thanks for your email – heavy irony and all.
    Best,
    * * * *

4

Faces in the Crowd
Dave's CD to Joanne – Tracklist

1. A Change Is Gonna Come – Sam Cooke
2. Waterfall – The Stone Roses
3. I've Just Seen a Face – The Beatles
4. High Tide or Low Tide – Bob Marley
5. Shipbuilding – Elvis Costello
6. A New England – Kirsty MacColl and Billy Bragg
7. Ten Storey Love Song – The Stone Roses
8. May You Never – John Martyn
9. Bankrobber – The Clash
10. Sunshine and Love – Happy Mondays
10. Angel – Jimi Hendrix
11. Cherish the Day – Sade
12. A Case of You – Joni Mitchell
13. I Want You – Bob Dylan
14. The Light Is Always Green – The Housemartins
15. Vice Versa Love – Barrington Levy
16. Silver Springs – Fleetwood Mac
17. It's Only Love – The Beatles
17. Sally Cinnamon (Live at the Hacienda '89)
The Stone Roses
18. Hallelujah/I Know It's Over (Live) – Jeff Buckley

5

I was flying out to Lagos with Ramin later on that day. I had just enough time to go to the Royal Court to deliver the first draft of *Faces in the Crowd*. I went up to the fifth floor and threw it on the literary manager's desk and made a speedy exit, I wanted to avoid anyone asking 'Are you pleased with it?'

In the end I flew out to Lagos on my own as Ramin had somehow missed the flight. It was an overnight trip so I should have had plenty of time to rest, but instead I was glued to the in-flight entertainment console with *The Departed* and *The Simpsons Movie* for company until the early hours of the morning. On arrival, after a stressful couple of hours waiting at baggage reclaim, I was met outside the heavily guarded airport by a British Council driver who bustled me into a bullet-proof van and took me to the hotel.

They told me I must never leave the hotel without an armed escort, and I told them I'd been here before and that I knew what I was doing. The group of twelve local playwrights would be arriving later. They'd finished their drafts and we were going to spend the next ten days developing them so there was plenty to be getting on with. The British Council had booked one of the hotel's conference rooms for us to work in and so – once I'd checked in – I decided to have a nose around. After peering into our conference room, I went to the reception telling them that we didn't need all the decorated tables or the podiums or the microphones. A dozen plastic chairs, some paper and pens, and a football would be fine.

Once that was sorted I went to the restaurant to have some break-fast. Unfortunately, it was empty, they weren't serving anything at the moment, but the waiter did say I could help myself to some corn-flakes. I spooned the cornflakes into the kiddy-sized bowl and asked if the waiter could bring me some milk. I had a bottle of water with me so I took my first malaria tablet of the day and checked my mobile phone for a signal. I was dying to call home, as well as wondering if the literary manager might leave a message to say that she'd picked up my play yesterday. There was no signal so I decided to do some planning for the next day's workshop instead. I still wasn't sure if Ramin would get another flight in time to join me, so I decided to plan a couple of sessions that I knew I could run by myself. Ball games, a bit of debriefing, discussion about our hopes and ambitions for the rest of the workshop, etc. It must have been twenty or thirty minutes later when the waiter returned with a saucer of powdered milk. I shouted at him and he went to away to fetch some actual milk, and then I felt bad for shouting at him.

I was bored now. I went to my room, unwrapped a pack of duty-free Camel Lights and made myself a coffee with the jar of Nescafé I'd bought at the airport. I thought I'd go outside and read some of the writers' scripts. It was almost midday and the sun was coming out. There were two or three middle-aged white blokes on sunbeds and four or five young black girls swimming in the pool. One of the girls climbed out and took a seat next to me. After she complimented my eyes and hair for a few moments I suddenly realised that I was being approached by a prostitute. I thanked her for the compliments, gave it another ten minutes then went quietly back inside.

The white guys, it turned out, were there for a Shell business conference, and it was routine for the company to provide them with young women during their stay. I decided to watch TV. I found an American show which had Wallace Shawn in a funny little cameo part. My mind started to wander, thinking about *Designated Mourner*, how inconceivable that it's written by Rex from *Toy Story*, and I gradually fell asleep.

It must have been late afternoon when I woke up. The sun was blasting through the window. I climbed off the bed and decided to check around the skirting boards and behind the cupboards for any spiders or bugs.

Then I made another coffee to wake myself up and checked my phone to see if there was any news about Ramin. It was a relief to find that there was a tiny bit of a signal in the room if you stood in the right place, and, to my surprise, someone had left me a voicemail.

A moment later I was listening to the literary manager of the Royal Court telling me she'd read *Faces in the Crowd* and that it was good news.

I sat down on the bed and plugged in my laptop to play some music.

6

Prop List – Limerick 1760. Abject Poverty

No.	Scene	Item	Character	Notes	Have Actual
	Scene 1				
Scenic	Scene 1	Standing Stocks/Pillory	Dermot		
1	Scene 1	Stool	Ellen		
2	Scene 1	Bucket with water	Ellen	For washing Dermot's feet	
3	Scene 1	Cloth	Ellen	For washing Dermot's feet	
	Scene 2				
Scenic	Scene 2	Plank Bed	Mud Cabin	Tree stump legs to kick out	
4	Scene 2	Old Blankets	Maryanne – on bed		
5	Scene 2	Stool	Maryanne		
6	Scene 2	Tripod	Maryanne	Over fire with hook for pot	
7	Scene 2	Pot with Potato Stew	Maryanne	On Tripod	
8	Scene 2	Kitchen & eating utensils/ implements	Mud Cabin		
9	Scene 2	Hessian Sack	L. Ryan		
10	Scene 2, Pg 9	Severed Pig Head	L. Ryan	In Hessian sack (item 11)	
Armoury	Scene 2	Sword	L. Coyle		*
11	Scene 2, Pg 16	Dead Chicken to pluck	Ellen		*
12	Scene 2, Pg 17	Dead Chicken to pluck	Maryanne		*
13	Scene 2, Pg 21	Slaughtered Pig	Ryan	In sack with head out	
14	Scene 2, Pg 25	Drinking Flask	Ryan		
Armoury	Scene 2, Pg 25	Dagger	Coyle		
Wardrobe	Scene 2, Pg 33	Crucifix on Chain	Ellen	Gets ripped off Coyle Sc 3	
15	Scene 2, Pg 35	Missal	Ellen	Fits in her pocket	
16	Scene 2, Pg 35	Ladle	Maryanne		
17	Scene 2, Pg 35	Small Bowl	Maryanne	For Stew	
18	Scene 2, Pg 42	Purse	L. Coyle		

19	Scene 2, Pg 42	Twenty Guineas	L. Coyle	For Purse (item 21)	
	Scene 3				
20	Scene 3	Table 1500 - 1200mm long	Tavern	To sit 6 comfortably	
21	Scene 3	1 x Bench	Tavern	For long table (item 23)	
22	Scene 3	Small Table	Tavern	To sit 2 -4 people	
23	Scene 3	2 x Chairs	Tavern		
24	Scene 3	Wooden crates	Tavern	For carrying bottles or sat on	
25	Scene 3	Candles in holders	Tavern		
26	Scene 3	Bar equipment and utensils	Tavern	Incl. Spit utensils	
27	Scene 3	Spit equipment, tongs, skewer	Tavern		
28	Scene 3	Regimental flag and Union Jack	Tavern	Dressing	
39	Scene 3	Portrait of King George III	Tavern		
30	Scene 3	Cups with drink	Tavern/Pot Boy		
31	Scene 3	Jug for serving drink	Pot Boy		
32	Scene 3	Dead Piglet	Dermot		
33/Armoury	Scene 3	Blunt Knife	Dermot	Home made job that's penknife like	
34	Scene 3	Ankle Shackles	Dermot	Unlocked but fastened	
35	Scene 3	Bit of a tree	Dermot	Attached by shackles (item36)	
36	Scene 3	Drink (?) Ale (?)	Tavern		
Wigs	Scene 3, Pg 51	Piss	C. Farrell	Pisses in Dermot's cup. Dermot drinks	
Armoury	Scene 3	5 x Swords	soldiers		
Wigs	Scene 3, Pg 73	Blood	Dermot	After beating by soldiers	
37	Scene3, Pg 86	Pipe	C. O'Connor	Given to L. Ryan	
Wigs	Scene 3, Pg 89	Blood	Pot Boy	Bleeding to death	
Wigs	Scene 3, Pg 94	Piss	C. Farrell	Pisses on Missal	
	Scene 4				
38	Scene 4, Pg 98	Soup	Ellen	Made with pigs blood	
39/Armoury	Scene 4, Pg 109	Blade (same as item 35)	Dermot	Stabs L.C. Finnegan	
40	Scene 4,	Padlock and key	Maryanne	For Dermot's	

	Pg 111			chains	
Wigs	Scene 4, Pg 113	2 x eyeballs	Dermot	Gauged from own head	
	Scene 5				
41	Scene 5	Candles and holders (?)	Fleming's ¼'s		
42	Scene 5	Parchment	Cl. Fleming	To be referred to	
43	Scene 5, Pg 121	Scroll	Capt. Farrell		
	Scene 6				
44	Scene 6, Pg 124	Drinking flask (different from item 16)	Cl. Fleming	Removes from pocket	
45	Scene 6, Pg 130	Shovel	L. Ryan		
Set	Scene 6, Pg 131	Soil	Cabin	To fill the hole	
46	Scene 6, Pg 133	Purse (different from item	Cl. Fleming		
47	Scene 6, Pg 133	Coins	Cl. Fleming	For purse (item 49)	
	Scene 7				
48	Scene 7, Pg 139	Hunk of bread	Ellen	To fit in pocket	
49	Scene 7, Pg 140	Bloody cloth	Ellen	From Dermot's feet	

7

'How's it going?'

'Great, yeah, just . . .'

'Well we're doing this thing where we want to put these mini-plays all over the building. It'll be ticketed but it's free, and anyone can just walk in and go on a sort of treasure hunt searching for plays that we've hidden, and we'll mix it up with new and established writers, so it doesn't feel too . . .'

'Yeah.'

'Yeah, and they'll each be about twenty minutes long and we'll record them with David and Ned here and . . . I don't know, try and make them available as a podcast at some point too.'

'Cool.'

'Yeah, so you don't have to think of it as a radio play, but we'll record them like a radio play, and the audience will look around and they'll find a play in, I don't know. Vicky's office or on the stairs or in the toilets. We'll give out clues of course, it'll be fun, and there'll be a set of headphones in each of the locations and, basically, the plays will be running on a loop and the audience can stop and put on the headphones, listen to the whole thing or . . . not, depending on . . .'

'Could I do one for the balcony overlooking Sloane Square?'

'Sure, yeah, that'd be cool, and you might want to think about the kind of thing that'll work well in that space. It's about giving the audience a different kind of experience, challenging the way we think about "what makes a theatrical space" and the relationship between the play and the spectator. Do you want to go away and have a think about it?'

8

ROYAL COURT THEATRE   SHOW REPORT

SHOW Faces in the Crowd   **Jerwood Theatre Downstairs**

DATE: 07.11.08   **PERFORMANCE: 22**

HOUSE: 73

	Lights up	Lights down	Playing time	Running time
Part One	19:50	21:19	1hr 29	1hr 29

SM: Nicola Chisholm   **LX Op:**

SM: Ruth Murfit   **Sound Op:**

Duty LX: Emily   **Duty Carpenter:§Charles Ash**

Duty House Manager: Claire Simpson

COMMENTS

1. Mr O'Neill banged his shin on the side of the bed as he was climbing in, adding a 'Bollocks'. DSM checked with him after the show and he is not injured.

Two calls were taken.

9

This was my second trip to Nigeria in the space of twelve months, all part of the theatre's commitment to discovering international work which has been led by the indefatigable Elyse Dodgson for the last twenty-five years or so. Elyse usually teams a playwright up with a director, such as Ramin, and sends them off to work with a dozen promising new writers in, say, Chile or Zimbabwe. After a couple of weeks' intensive workshops and some very competitive ball-games, there may – and very often is – a play or playwright that the Royal Court goes on to produce. And, as there aren't many writers who can earn a living from playwriting alone, to get paid to travel to somewhere like Nigeria, during their summer and our winter, is not to be sniffed at.

Although the British Council had forbidden us to leave the hotel complex, we did sneak out a couple of times. Once, in the daytime, when Ramin wanted to find somewhere to get a haircut, and again, at night, when I went out with one of our writers, Ozi, to get some meat. We'd sneaked through the hotel's security gates and Ozi flagged down a couple of young kids on rusty yellow mopeds. Clinging on to our drivers, we bounced dangerously along the busy potholed highways until we reached the vast, late-night market lit up with fires from the scores of charred oil drums. Five minutes later, we climbed back aboard the mopeds and headed back to the hotel with two plastic bags weighed down with hot sizzling meat. The ride was exhilarating, and the meat tasted okay, but our hosts were furious. In fact, when it came to my third and final trip, twelve months later, the British Council made us work in the back of their offices so that they could keep an eye on us. Clare Lizzimore was the director that time, and we'd just worked together on the production of *Faces in the Crowd*. It really didn't seem like a year since I was with Ramin at the Africa Shrine, preparing for the production of *I'll Be the Devil* for the Royal Shakespeare Company. And it was only two years ago that I'd had my very first visit to Lagos, with Elyse and Hettie Macdonald. During that trip we'd met local director/choreographer Odey Anthony, whose company had treated us to an incredible display of contemporary dance set to tribal drumming. Elyse and I were so impressed that, only a few months later, I was working with

Odey at the Royal Court, collaborating on *Airbag*. I remember Odey was delighted when I arrived to rehearsals with a jar of Nescafé I'd brought from home.

10

I'd like to credit a few people who supported, inspired and helped bring these plays to life.

Ramin Gray, Clare Lizzimore, Donnacadh O'Briain, George Perrin, Odey Anthony, Ned Bennett, Elyse Dodgson, Dominic Cooke, Jeanie O'Hare, Michael Boyd, Clare McQuillan, Carissa Hope Lynch, Emily McLaughlin, Ruth Little, Howard Gooding, Anna Brewer, the late great Gerard Murphy, the sorely missed David McLennan, and all the casts and crews of the shows.

I'd also like to thank all the brilliant playwrights I had the pleasure to teach and to work with at the Royal Court, and in Lagos, South Africa, Zimbabwe and Chile.

Finally, I'd like to thank my family and, in particular, Nazzi and Bea, for being there through thick and thin.

Airbag

Airbag was first performed at the Royal Court Theatre, London, as part of the Rough Cuts season, on 2 July 2007, with the following cast and creative team:

Mrs Gorman   Gillian Hanna
Lisa   Nicola Walker
Joe   Nick Moss
Dancers/Musicians   Vincent Etagweyo, Frank Asiyai and Odey Anthony

Director Leo Butler
Choreographer Odey Anthony

Characters

Mrs Gorman, *elderly and frail*
Joe, *forties*
Lisa, *forties*

Setting

A bed.

The text is deliberately written with wide gaps between lines.
These can be filled with silence, or with movement/dance.

One

Mrs Gorman, *elderly and frail, is sitting at the end of the bed.*

Mrs Gorman　Gorilla.

Gorilla, look.

Gorilla tapping at the window.

At this time of night?

I mean, we've had cats before.

They come in over the back wall don't they, Billy? There's that lovely strawberry blonde from number twelve, he's quite the charmer.

Often leave 'im a saucer of milk.

Saucer of milk, a small slice of something. Fill his belly at least, a scrap of chicken from the roast.

Nothing like this though, mind.

No gorillas, I mean.

Dark black eyes peeping through the ivy, peeping through at me.

Do you think it's cold out there?

Do you think I should offer him a blanket of something?
Something to keep the rain off his back.

Billy.

Wake up, Billy.

Billy, please.

Come on now, child, listen to your grandmother.

Do you think it's cold out there?

You can hear me, can't you?

Fat leathery fingers beating at the glass, don't encourage 'im!

Don't encourage him, you'll only wind him up!

Shut the curtains.

Shut the curtains, he'll see you.

He'll see us both, get down.

How many?

How many exactly?

Oh.

Oh, well, I suppose they can't mean any harm by it.

It's probably just him and his friends, they can't possibly . . .

I suppose they just got lost.

They got lost on their way to the hospital, look.

Look again, open the curtains.

Look again, Billy, he's looking through my nightgown.

He's looking in at me through my nightgown, the devil.
He's lucky I don't call the police.

He's lucky I don't call the RSPCA, the devil. Looking me up and
down, my best nightgown.

My best nightgown, in this heat.

At my age.

At my age, Billy, aren't you going to say something?

You're not a baby any more, come on.

Come on, Billy, tell them they've got the wrong house, tell them . . .

Tell them they can take their party elsewhere. 'You're not welcome,
I said! It's gone midnight, you animals, there's people trying to
sleep!'

There's people trying to sleep, Billy, well?

I mean . . .

I mean I've had about a hundred bloody cats before now. All the years I've lived here, all the years.

All the years, Billy, tell them. Tell them we're not looking for any trouble, tell them to go next door, they'll know what to do. Tell them to call the police, the Samaritans – give them directions, Billy, please!

If it's food they want.

If it's food, if it's something I've done to upset them.

If you've upset them.

Billy?

If this is one of your pranks, if these are friends of yours.
If your fucking mother were here, all the years.
All the years, smashing the glass.

Smashing the glass.

Smashing the glass, breaking the locks.
They're climbing in through the walls, child.

Billy, please – there's how many? There's how many now? Please, tell them to stop!

They're coming for us, Billy, they're coming through, wake up!

Through the window.

Through the window . . .

Two

Lisa *and* **Joe** *sitting at opposite sides of the bed.* **Lisa** *speaks,* **Joe** *does not.*

Lisa   Thought you'd prefer it by the window.

You've got a good view of the park, look.

All the old trees. The playground.

You'll be able to wave to us when we take the dogs out.

Joe's going to take them out every morning he says. Every morning before work.

That's good of him, isn't it?

It's good they let him work from home, I mean.

That's good though isn't it, Mum? All of us together.

Back where you belong. You and me.

Just me and you, alright?

Alright, Mum?

Back at home together. All of us this time, you hear me?

You can hear me can't you?

Course you're tired.

I mean, you're bound to be tired. All that pushing and shoving. Getting you up the stairs, all that effort, all those flights.

You're just bound to be fucking . . .

I put your pictures on the cabinet, look.

I lined them all up just as you like them.

I mean, you're going to want to see them all aren't you? There's no point keeping them at that . . .

At that place still, not until you can . . .

I did it for you, look.

I did it for you, Mum, look.

It was me, you hear? I did it all.

That's right though, isn't it, Joe?

There's some photos of the kids I could frame for you.

There's one of Billy from his swimming gala. He's the sweetest little pigeon in his speedos, you have to see it.

I could frame it and put it with the others couldn't I?

Give you something to smile about.

Makes me smile at least.

Makes me laugh my fucking head off it does. Doesn't it you, Mum?

Mum.

Doesn't it make you laugh though? Be honest.

Be honest, come on.

Be honest for once in your fucking life.

We could ask him to come and read his comics for you.

Billy, I mean.
I'm sure he wouldn't mind.

Any excuse to not . . .

Any excuse to spend some time away from . . .

From his father, I mean. Any bloody excuse.

You'd like that wouldn't you, Mum?

He's done nothing but ask about you, poor thing.
Poor little bean, he's been up every night with worry.

You'd like that wouldn't you?

Keeping you company, well?

Well.

You can tell me later on then, can't you?

Tell me what you'd like, if there's anything you need.

If there's anything else I can bring up for you, anything at all, Mum.

If there's anything I . . .

I can do, if I . . .

I

If there's anything I . . .

Eaten away.

Eating away inside you, old bag.

Cancerous old bag, you're doing this on purpose. You're doing this to me – Well, aren't you?

Can't you hear me?

You know we're all praying for you.

That's right though isn't it, Joe?

We're all praying for you, Mum.

Mum, please . . .

Three

Mrs Gorman *sitting at the end of the bed.*

Please, don't . . .

Don't let them see you, I said, stay down.

Stay down, Billy, keep your head under the pillow, go on.

Go on will you? – The dirty thieving apes, look.
The dirty drooling jackals, as they're breaking through the walls.

Breaking through the walls, the plaster, as they're biting through the brick, the bastards.

'Haven't you had enough?!'

At this time of night, in this weather.

At this time of . . .

Wake up, Billy — 'Haven't you had enough fun for one night?! I'll call the police, I'll call the bloody zoo!' 'Don't come near us, I said, you'll have his mother to answer to! You'll have the end of my stick, you hear?!' Hands on my chest.

Hands on my chest.

Hands on my throat, they're choking . . . .

The dirt from the garden with their hands on my throat.

Hands through my nightgown, the one you . . .

The one the doctors brought.

The one they bought, the one she – My nightgown.

My nightgown, with their fingers, their fat hairy fingers. – Their fingers on my skin. 'Get off me I said, get off!'

Devil.

Hairy devil inside.

Inside me, Billy, hide.

Get under the pillow. don't . . .

Don't let them see you, Billy, stay down.

Running down my legs.

Their filth. Their sticky white filth running down my legs – there's how many?

In and out, in and out – There's how many now?

In and out. in and out.

Dirty drooling jackals, him and his friends –- on my throat, through the nightgown. In and out.

In and out.

What are they building down there?

They're building something.

I can feel it, Billy, listen.

Gorillas.

Teeming with gorillas.

Practically teeming, up up inside.

Pitching their tent in my belly, all the way.
All the way now, multiplying.
Positively teeming.
A thousand terrible silverbacks.

What are they building down there?

What are they building down there, tell me!

'You've had your fun for one night, you're hurting me, stop!'

Hands on my throat, they're inside, the beasts, listen!

Billy?

Can't you hear them?

Tell me you can hear them, Billy.

Billy . . .

Four

Joe *and* **Lisa** *sitting at opposite sides of the bed, facing each other.*
Lisa *speaks,* **Joe** *doesn't.*

Lisa   Billy will pray for you.

Can't you hear me?

He'll do that for you, I promise.

He will.

Yes he will, he's with his uncle as we speak.
They've gone to see the reverend, Mum, don't you worry.

That's right though isn't it, Joe?

We'll pray to the Lord Jesus Christ.

You do remember Jesus don't you?
In the stories.

In the stories, Mum, remember, the ones you used to . . .

The ones you made me promise . . .

We'll pray together, look.

I mean, what do they know?

What do they know? — I mean, really.

Better to be at home with us.
Better with your own, out of that fucking . . .

That fucking place. God forgive me.

Forgive me.

God forgive me.

You can forgive me, can't you?

I'll put his picture on the cabinet, look.

Little Billy.

Little Billy-boy.

I'll put it on the bedside cabinet for you.
With the view through the window, you'd like that wouldn't you?

Tell me you'd like that, Mum.

Tell me you'd like me to do that for you.

My fucking debt to you, look, tell me!

The view of the park, look, set your mind at rest.

We'll pray together won't we, Joe?

Back at home where you belong.

Joe . . .

Joe   She's shit all over the sheets.

It's everywhere, Lisa.

Lisa . . .

Lisa   Don't.

Joe   What?

Don't what?

Lisa   I've told them already, don't . . .

Joe   It's rancid.

Lisa   What?

Joe   The smell's rancid, woman.

Don't you think you should have moved her?

Don't you think you should have checked the bed-sheets at least?

Don't you think you shouldn't have left it so late?

I'm asking you a question!

Lisa . . .

Lisa   Don't look at me like that, I know.

Joe   Blood and shit and God knows what.

Lisa   Alright, just . . .

Joe   How long has she been like this?

Lisa   Joe, please . . .

Joe   What have you been doing all day?

Lisa   Just leave it would you?!

Joe   She's not ready.

She's not ready for this. She should have stayed . . .

Lisa   She'll be back on her feet in no time.

Joe   Yeah . . .

Lisa   In no time at all, Joe, the doctor said . . .

Joe   Yeah, that's right . . .

Lisa   It's better that she's with us now.

Lisa   That's right though isn't it, Mum?

Lisa   All of us together.

Joe   Together . . .

Lisa   You don't have to stay.

What?

You don't have to do anything, Joe.

Joe   No . . .

Lisa   No, nothing you don't want to. Not if it's any inconvenience.

Joe   It's my bed.

Lisa   That's right.

Joe   It's our bed, Lisa.

Lisa   Mother . . .

Joe   She can't hear you.

Lisa   Mother . . .

Joe   Don't use this as one of your excuses!

Give me your hand.

Give me your hand, will you?

You know I don't mind.

I could build it.

Joe   I could build an extension, we could keep her . . .

In her own small . . .

It would be her own small room. I could knock a door through, you wouldn't have to . . .

I could borrow the tools from work. The materials, I could . . .

We could build it together.

We could do that, me and you.

We could keep her in the shed.

In the fucking garden or something, in the bushes.

In the bloody bushes, imagine!

Give me your hand, Lisa, please.

You know I don't mind.

The two of us together.

As it should be.

You and me, Lisa, the bitch.

In her shit.

In her piss and her shit.

She could watch.

She could watch you clean it all up, Lisa. She could take that with her.

Everyone takes something with them, don't they?

Lisa   Of course.

Of course, if we pray. If we pray for Jesus . . .

Jesus will take your soul.

Jesus will carry it through the window, he will.

That's what you promised, isn't it?

He'll carry it through the ozone layer.

Up through the atmosphere, up up and away.

With all the little angels – that's right, he will, even Billy knows that.

His picture on the cabinet, look.

At the swimming gala.

Little Billy . . .

Five

Mrs Gorman *sitting at the end of the bed.*

Can't you hear them, Billy?

In and out, in and out – through the window.

In and out – don't just lay there, child, wake up!

Wake up.

Wake up, Billy, look.

Gorilla.

Big beautiful gorilla, look. Him and his friends.
Can't you see them?
Can't you see what they've built?

Look.

Look again, look.

Look at me I said, wake up!

Alright, Billy, don't cry.

Don't cry, my sweetheart, don't cry.

Don't cry, I said.

Billy?

You remember, don't you?

I mean, we've had all the little kittens here before.

His strawberry blonde coat.

He'd smile at you and his face would break into a thousand tiny wrinkles.

Saucer of mik, a slice of—
That's right now, shhhh.

Shhhh.

That's it now, that's better.

That's it, my angel, you get your head down, I'm sorry I snapped.

At this time of night.

Through the window, at this time, look.

Lay your head on my shoulder, that's it.

That's it, Billy, through the window.

At this time of night, in this heat . . .

In this heat.

Of course you do get a very good view.

The park.

The trees, the playground.
Through the window, up up and away.

Up and away now, can't you see?

Can't you see, Billy? Look.

You can see the continent of Africa.

You can see it between the hours of ten and two.
That's the brightest part of the day.

Europe, look.

Asia at bedtime.

Don't worry, it'll be our little secret.

No.

No, of course I won't tell your mother.

The Americas.

The Far East.

All that oxygen.

All the beautiful oxygen, look.

I'll Be the Devil

I'll Be the Devil was first produced by the Royal Shakespeare Company and premiered at the Tricycle Theatre, London. on 21 February 2008, with the following cast and creative team:

Dermot	Tom Burke
Ellen	Samantha Young
Lieutenant Coyle	Eoin McCarthy
Maryanne	Derbhle Crotty
Lieutenant Ryan	Andrew Macklin
Sergeant Browne	Gerard Murphy
Captain Farrell	Edward MacLiam
Captain Skelton	JD Kelleher
Corporal O'Connor	Billy Carter
Lance Corporal Finnigan	Colm Gormley
Pot-Boy	David Toole
Colonel Fleming	John McEnery

Director Ramin Gray
Designer Lizzie Clachan
Lighting Designer Charles Balfour
Sound Designer Fergus O'Hare
Music Peter Cowdrey
Movement Anna Morrissey
Fights Philip d'Orleans
Assistant Director Jonathan Humphreys

Characters

Maryanne
Dermot, *Maryanne's son*
Ellen, *Maryanne's daughter*
Lieutenant Coyle, *Maryanne's lover*
Lieutenant Ryan, *Coyle's second*
Sergeant Browne
Captain Farrell
Captain Skelton
Corporal O'Connor
Lance Corporal Finnigan
Colonel Fleming, *an Englishman*
Pot-Boy
Fiddler
Piper

Setting

In and around Limerick, south-west Ireland. Two stormy nights approaching Easter, 1762.

The scenes should flow effortlessly into each other, punctuated by the storm. The play should be performed without an interval.

One

Dusk.

The hills.

Dermot *is placed in the stocks.*

It is a pillory, or 'standing stocks', resembling a crucifix. There is a small stool by the stocks.

Dermot's *eyes have been gouged out. His clothes are rags, and he is covered with dried blood, cuts and bruises.*

Ellen *is crouched by him. She has a bucket and a cloth. She is washing his feet and legs.*

Dermot   I saw the Devil last night, Ellen. He rode up out the Shannon on his horse. A great black Barbary she was, and him all burning red under his cloak. He asks me to sign his covenant with his claws pulled tight upon me throat. A dozen yellow eyes he has, a tongue the length of your arm. 'Not so long as I have breath in me head,' I says, 'Not so long as I can still draw blood. Get back under the earth,' I cry, 'and you take your stinking nag along with you!' Well, he didn't like that now, did he?

Ellen   No.

Dermot   He didn't like that.

Ellen   He didn't like that, no.

Dermot   Him all fallen from Heaven and I no better than ink without the pot, let alone the hand that drives it. Oh, the noise he made, Ellen. I swear he would've shook the Lord from off his cross had he sense enough to mark it, had I not been Saint of this rock. Had I not such a wealth of angels in me breast and not seen off his poison already.

Long pause.

Ellen.

Pause.

Ellen.

Ellen   Yes, Dermot?

Dermot   He spat in me ear, look.

Ellen   In your ear he spat?

Dermot   It was me brain he was aiming for.

Ellen   Oh.

Dermot   Can you not see?

Pause.

Ellen . . .

Ellen   It would take more than the Devil to clear a path through this filth.

Dermot   But I saw him, I tell you!

Ellen   And what would the Devil want with you?

Dermot   He thinks he has me fooled. He thinks he can drag me down through Purgatory.

Ellen   Oh, Dermot . . .

Dermot   The dirty beast.

Ellen   You're so stupid.

Dermot   You don't fool me, you old bastard, you can curse all you want! You can claw the flesh from off my bones for all the good it'll do you! You can choke on your own forked tongue, so help me God!

Long pause.

That'll teach him, won't it?

Pause.

That'll teach him though, won't it?

Pause.

Ellen . . .

A rumble of thunder. Long pause.

Ellen . . .

Ellen   Would you stop . . . ?

Dermot   Shhhh!

Ellen   Stop wiggling your feet.

Dermot   Do you not hear him?

Ellen   I hear nothing.

Dermot   Listen!

Ellen   Oh, Dermot, come on . . .

Dermot   He's calling us even now, my sister!

Ellen   I'll never clean off this blood if you don't keep still.

Dermot   But I swear to you, that's his mark.

Ellen   Keep still I say!

Dermot   Once he's shown himself the once, once he's found his way inside.

Ellen   Just calm down and let me . . .

Dermot   Tell me you'll pray for me, Ellen, please!

A burst of thunder. Long pause.

Ellen   Have you emptied your bladder yet?

Pause.

Do you need the bucket, Dermot?

Pause.

There's no need to sulk now.

Dermot   I'm not sulking.

Ellen   You want to look the best for Our Lord.

Dermot (*mimics* **Ellen**)   'You want to look the best for Our Lord.'

Ellen   You're lucky they never cut your tongue out. The state of you, look. Blind as a beetle.

Dermot   And whose fault is that?

Ellen   You want to make a good impression. Don't you want that?

Pause.

You'll only upset Mammy.

Pause.

Dermot . . .

Dermot   He asked after you.

Pause.

Ellen   Dermot, please . . .

Dermot   He asked after you, he did.

Ellen   Oh now –

Dermot   He did!

Ellen   Don't be so –

Dermot   He called you by name, he did. 'Fetch me the midget,' he says. 'Fetch me the girl.'

Ellen   Dermot . . .

Dermot   'Fetch me the dwarf won't listen when she's spoken to and I'll roast her on me spit.'

Ellen   Dermot, please . . .

Dermot   'I'll roast her like a pig, just you see that I don't!'

Ellen   That's enough.

Dermot   'A dirty little piggy-wig sucking on her own filth!'

Ellen   If you won't keep –

Dermot   Get your hands off me!

Ellen   That's enough now, Dermot –

Dermot   Stop haunting me, pig!

Ellen   But I'm only –

Dermot   Oink oink oink!

Ellen   I only want to –

Dermot   Oink oink oink oink oink!

Ellen *throws the bucket of dirty water at* **Dermot**'*s face.*

Long pause.

Dermot   Ellen . . .

Ellen   No.

Dermot   But you promised me, Ellen.

Ellen   I can't hear you.

Dermot   We have to believe –

Ellen   I can't hear you, Dermot, no!

Ellen *moves and sits on the grass, a distance apart from* **Dermot**.

Long pause.

Dermot   There is such a thing though, isn't there?

Pause.

You do believe me though, don't you, girl?

Long pause.

Ellen.

Thunder and lightning.

Ellen, please.

It starts to rain.

I don't know what to believe.

Blackout.

Two

A mud cabin, built within the woods.

Night.

The storm, outside — thunder, lightning, heavy rain. Though the cabin has a roof, it cannot stop the rain from pouring in.

Maryanne *is sitting on the stool by the peat fire, plucking a chicken.*

Lieut Coyle *is standing by the open doorway. He is joined by* **Lieut Ryan**. *He carries an old hessian sack, in which is something big and heavy.*

Lieut Coyle   Where is he?

Maryanne   You're late.

Lieut Coyle   Don't play games with me now.

Maryanne   Oh, God forbid –

Lieut Coyle   I've warned you about that boy of yours.

Maryanne   – that I should quarrel with the palatine.

Lieut Coyle   Where is he?

Maryanne   You're letting the rain in.

Lieut Coyle   If you think I'm going to stand here . . .

Maryanne   Stand here like a mule can't hold his own piss.

Lieut Coyle   I'm warning you, Maryanne . . .

Maryanne   Shut the fucking door why don't you?!

Lieut Coyle *slams the door shut.*

Pause.

Lieut Coyle   Is that all right for you, lady of the house?

Maryanne   Fine.

Lieut Coyle   Do you mind if I take a look around?

Maryanne   Be my guest.

Lieut Coyle *doesn't move.*

Pause.

Maryanne   Is something the matter, Lieutenant?

Lieut Coyle   You know, you could save yourself a lot of time . . .

Maryanne   What?

Lieut Coyle   You could save yourself a lot of trouble . . .

Maryanne   You'll have to speak up, sir – what?

Lieut Coyle   If you would just tell me . . .

Maryanne   Dumb bastard, you.

Lieut Coyle   Are you trying to ruin me, woman?!

He throws the hessian sack on **Maryanne**'s *lap.*

Lieut Coyle   I should rip his rotten eyes out!

Maryanne (*peers into the sack*)   Is this for me, sir?

Lieut Coyle   In God's name . . .

Maryanne   Now you know I can't accept donations.

Lieut Coyle   Maryanne . . .

Maryanne   I suggest you seek indulgence elsewhere.

Lieut Coyle   Maryanne, please . . .

Maryanne   Preferably your arse.

Pause.

Lieut Coyle   Did you put him up to this?

Maryanne   She is a beauty, sir.

Lieut Coyle   What?

Maryanne   Oh yes, I can certainly see the resemblance.

She pulls a pig's severed head out of the sack.

One of your Londonderry cousins, I'm thinking.

Lieut Coyle   All right now, just –

Maryanne   One of your clan.

Lieut Coyle   Maryanne . . .

Maryanne   Is she Catholic or Protestant, I wonder?

Lieut Coyle   I didn't come here to be mocked.

Maryanne   What do you say, pig?

Lieut Coyle   I'm warning you now.

Maryanne   Are you a papal pig?

Lieut Coyle   Look . . .

Maryanne   Perhaps she'd care to take communion, sir.

Lieut Coyle   If they find him . . .

Maryanne   What's it to be?

Lieut Coyle   If he so much as mentions my name!

Maryanne   Would you like that, pig?

Lieut Coyle   Do you know who this belonged to?!

He grabs the pig's head from **Maryanne**.

Lieut Coyle   Do you know?!

Maryanne   Now steady on, Lieutenant . . .

Lieut Coyle   Jesus save us!

Maryanne   There's no need to shout.

Lieut Coyle   I told you he's not to go near that farm!

Maryanne   And whose farm might that be, sir?

Lieut Coyle   You know what I'm talking about.

Maryanne   The farm you stole from me?

Lieut Coyle   It belongs to the military now.

Maryanne   The holy fucking surge.

Lieut Coyle   You know that, Maryanne, please!

Long pause.

Maryanne . . .

Maryanne   Yes, I see, sir, of course.

Lieut Coyle   Did you not tell him?!

Maryanne   I understand, sir.

Lieut Coyle   You've told him before what would happen.

Maryanne   The farm your Colonel obtained.

Lieut Coyle   You've warned him not to leave your side, you've done so.

Maryanne   The farm . . .

Lieut Coyle   The farm he's ransacked, woman!

Maryanne   The farm still reeks of my family's own blood.

Lieut Coyle   Take a look if you don't believe me! There are cattle scattered all over the land, Maryanne. Slaughtered, sodomised cattle – who else but that fucking lunatic?! Who else would do a thing like that – disfigured by the boy's own blade?! The stench itself would wake the dead, it's beyond human, Maryanne, he did this!

Pause.

Lieut Coyle   Maryanne . . .

Maryanne   You're foaming, Lieutenant.

Lieut Coyle (*wipes his mouth*)   You have to find him.

Maryanne   Do I?

Lieut Coyle   You have to find him and bring him home.

Maryanne   Is that an order?

Lieut Coyle   He's not to break the curfew.

Maryanne   You're threatening me.

Lieut Coyle   He's not to leave your side, that's the law.

Maryanne   Under whose authority?

Lieut Coyle   It's been the law for these past twenty years, woman, are you telling me it just slipped your mind?

Maryanne   Oh, then I must be punished, sir.

Lieut Coyle   What?

Maryanne   I see you've brought the fucking cavalry.

Pause.

Maryanne (*winks at* **Ryan**)   I clearly must be punished, sir, yes?

Lieut Coyle *hands the severed pig's head to* **Lieut Ryan**, *who exits, taking the pig's head with him.*

Maryanne   Of course I had hoped we might spend the evening together.

Lieut Coyle   For God's sake . . .

Maryanne   That we may keep each other warm, no?

Lieut Coyle   Is this any time . . . ?

Maryanne   Being only three days till Lent.

Lieut Coyle   What?

Maryanne   Penitence, sir. You will be joining in the fast, I trust?

Lieut Coyle   If you think I'm going to stand here and take orders . . .

Maryanne   It is the duty of every Catholic to forsake his belly over Easter.

Lieut Coyle   Maryanne . . .

Maryanne   You will be joining in the fast, sir.

Lieut Coyle   Where is he?

Maryanne   'Then was Jesus led into the wilderness to be tempted by the Devil. And when he had fasted forty days and forty nights, he was – '

Lieut Coyle   Maryanne, don't . . .

Maryanne   ' – afterward all hungered. And when the tempter came to – '

Lieut Coyle   For the love of God, don't do this to me!

Long pause.

Yes.

Maryanne   What?

Lieut Coyle   Yes, of course. Don't doubt my faith, Maryanne.

Maryanne   You were meant to be here three days ago.

Lieut Coyle   Look –

Maryanne   You laid your very life on it, sir.

Lieut Coyle   I haven't come here to –

Maryanne   Stuck in this hole without one scrap to call me own.

Lieut Coyle   And I am sorry, all right?

Maryanne   Without a single root to feed our children.

Lieut Coyle   I apologise, woman, can't you see – ?

Maryanne   You swore on the cross, Thomas!

Lieut Coyle   I have a regiment to keep, I can't just slip away –

Maryanne   Well, didn't you?!

Pause.

Lieut Coyle   Maryanne, please . . .

Maryanne   Under the bed.

Lieut Coyle   For Christ's sake, you're not even –

Maryanne   Under the bed, go on.

Lieut Coyle   I'm begging you –

Maryanne   Don't hurt my feelings now.

Lieut Coyle   Look at me, I'm –

Maryanne   The bed, go on!

Lieut Coyle *marches to the bed.*

Maryanne   Fat old Sassenach.

Lieut Coyle *frantically searches the blankets on the bed.*

Maryanne   Stick your head under.

Lieut Coyle   But –

Maryanne   Underneath, I said.

Lieut Coyle   There's nothing down there!

He overturns the bed. Long pause.

There's nothing down there.

Maryanne   Are you feeling better now, sir?

Lieut Coyle   Jesus Christ . . .

Maryanne   You should watch you don't injure yourself.

Lieut Coyle   Maryanne, don't . . .

Maryanne   A man of your standing.

Lieut Coyle   Don't make me . . .

Maryanne   A man of your weight.

Lieut Coyle   For the love of God!

Maryanne   You want to mind you don't damage your poor heart.

Lieut Coyle   Maryanne, please . . .

Maryanne   Fifty of your men come bursting through that door.

Lieut Coyle   Just let me talk to him.

Maryanne   I'd hate to be the one has to dig the fucking hole.

The storm blasts the cabin door open — crash!

Lieut Coyle *jumps, drawing his sword.*

He moves to the door and slams it shut, barring it with the bed.

Long pause.

Maryanne   Of course he won't be far away.

Lieut Coyle   What?

Maryanne   No, he won't stray too far, sir. He's no better than a dog when it comes to feeding, I'm sure you won't have to wait too long.

Pause.

Lieutenant . . .

Lieut Coyle   No.

Maryanne   You're not in any hurry, are you?

Pause.

Lieutenant, sir . . .

Lieut Coyle   I just told you, I'm not going anywhere, no! Dear God, woman, can you not answer a simple question?! I warned you before not to let him go out scavenging on his own, the matter was settled! I counted at least twenty dead pigs just now, he'll have us all in our graves if they catch him.

Maryanne   I should take that as a no then.

Lieut Coyle   He'll send us both to the hangman, don't you see? The Catholic is no better than a worm to those fiends, Maryanne. If he breathes one word, if they were to uncover my faith, if they discover my loyalty to you –

Maryanne   You call this loyalty!

Lieut Coyle   If they were to find the two of us here together like this. If they were to affiliate me with that madman.

Maryanne   Now that's no way to talk about the boy.

Lieut Coyle   The boy's an animal.

Maryanne   Your own son.

Lieut Coyle   He's no son of mine.

Maryanne   Well, I don't think —

Lieut Coyle   Not any more.

Maryanne   I don't think you have that choice, sir. Your children will bear your own coffin, I warrant, by spirit or by flesh.

Lieut Coyle   You know the rules, Maryanne.

Ellen (*hidden*)   Yes, sir.

Lieut Coyle   What?

Ellen (*hidden*)   Quite so, sir, yes.

Lieut Coyle   Are you . . . ?

Pause.

Are you trying to fucking . . . ?

Ellen (*hidden*)   Since you put it that way, sir —

Lieut Coyle *lifts up* **Maryanne**'s *skirt.* **Ellen** *is crouched between* **Maryanne**'s *legs, plucking a dead chicken.*

Ellen   I'm only too happy to oblige . . .

Lieut Coyle *drags* **Ellen** *out.*

Ellen   Ow!

Lieut Coyle   Would you look at the state of her?!

Ellen   Daddy, please!

Lieut Coyle   Jesus Christ . . .

Ellen   You're hurting me!

Lieut Coyle (*to* **Maryanne**)   Don't you have any decency?!

Ellen   Daddy . . .

Lieut Coyle (*to* **Maryanne**)   Well, don't you?!

Ellen   Daddy, please, my arm! Daddy . . .

Lieut Coyle (*to* **Maryanne**)   She's head to foot with it, look!

Maryanne *has returned to her stool, plucking the chicken.*

Lieut Coyle   I am addressing you, woman.

Maryanne   Oh come now, Lieutenant, it was only a bit of fun . . .

Lieut Coyle   Filth and mud and God knows what other excrement!

Ellen   Daddy, please, you're twisting my arm!

Lieut Coyle (*to* **Ellen**)   Look at me.

Ellen   It's hurting now, I can't . . .

Lieut Coyle (*to* **Ellen**)   Look at me, Ellen, give me your hand.

Ellen   But I thought you'd be pleased . . .

Lieut Coyle   Give me your hand now, come on.

He takes **Ellen** *by the hand and gets down on his knees.*

Lieut Coyle   Look to me, child.

Ellen   But I didn't mean –

Lieut Coyle   Look me in the eyes.

Ellen   But I didn't mean to make you so –

Lieut Coyle   Have you seen your brother? – Don't turn away now, come on.

Maryanne (*plucking her chicken*)   You're scaring the poor girl.

Lieut Coyle   Don't you lie to me now. You've seen him, haven't you?

Maryanne   Leave her alone, you big bully.

Lieut Coyle   Don't look to your mother — haven't I taught you not to tell tales?

Ellen   Yes, Daddy.

Lieut Coyle   Have I not taught you to follow the example of your patron saint?

Ellen   I know my place, Daddy, yes.

Lieut Coyle   Look at me.

Ellen   But I haven't –

Lieut Coyle   Look at me, Ellen, God help you!

He slaps **Ellen**.

Long pause.

Lieut Coyle   Ellen . . .

Ellen *starts to cry.*

Pause.

Lieut Coyle   Ellen, please, come on now, don't cry.

Pause.

Don't cry, Ellen . . .

Ellen (*crying*)   Get off me!

Lieut Coyle   Look –

Ellen (*crying*)   Get off me!

Lieut Coyle   You know I didn't mean to hurt —

Ellen (*crying*)   No!

Lieut Coyle   Oh, darling.

Ellen (*crying*)   I don't know what you're talking about.

Lieut Coyle   Come here.

Ellen (*crying*)   Daddy, no!

Lieut Coyle *locks* **Ellen** *in an embrace.*

Lieut Coyle   Come here, come on.

Lieut Coyle *kisses* **Ellen**'s *head.*

Lieut Coyle   That's it now. That's better.

Pause.

Daddy kiss it better.

Ellen   But I don't . . .

Lieut Coyle   Poor sweetheart.

Ellen (*crying*)   But I don't know what you mean . . .

Lieut Coyle   Poor mite, come here.

Ellen (*crying*)   I haven't seen anyone on the cross, I haven't.

Lieut Coyle   I know, darling, I know.

Ellen (*crying*)   I wanted to surprise you, Mammy said –

Lieut Coyle   I know, I'm sorry.

Ellen (*crying*)   Mammy said we were to give you a welcome home.

Lieut Coyle   Yes, and you've done so, Ellen . . .

Ellen (*crying*)   That I might help cheer you. That I might sit you down by the fire and help to dry you off from the storm.

Lieut Coyle   Oh, my darling, you know that I wouldn't –

Ellen (*crying*)   That we might pray together for Easter.

Lieut Coyle   And we will, Ellen, we will, come on now, please. You know I wouldn't dream of hurting you, don't you?

Ellen *cries.*

Lieut Coyle   You know that, don't you, girl?

He kisses **Ellen**.

Lieut Coyle   You know that deep down?

Ellen (*crying*)   Yes, Daddy.

Lieut Coyle   'For in thee, O Lord, do I put my trust: let me never be put to confusion. Deliver me in thy righteousness and cause me to escape: incline thine ear unto me, and save me.'

Pause.

You remember the verse I taught your brother and you both?

Ellen   Yes, of course.

Lieut Coyle   'For thou . . . '

Ellen   'For thou art my rock and salvation.'

Lieut Coyle   Then you remember the oaths we took.

Ellen   Yes, I know, but –

Lieut Coyle   Then you can forgive me, can't you?

Ellen   But I didn't –

Lieut Coyle   Say you'll forgive me, darling.

Maryanne (*plucking her chicken*)   Oh, she forgives you all right. She'll forgive the very Devil, won't you, girl?

Lieut Coyle   Say it, Ellen, for the love of God.

Maryanne   I would place her among the saints were I pontiff.

Lieut Coyle (*embraces* **Ellen**)   Ellen, please . . .

Maryanne   The virtue in her.

Lieut Coyle   Say that you forgive your father.

Maryanne   Though Christ knows where she gets it.

Lieut Coyle (*to* **Maryanne**)   Would you stop . . . ?

Maryanne   I often wonder if she fell from Heaven, sir.

Lieut Coyle   I'm talking to her!

Maryanne   Coming from your spineless cock –

Lieut Coyle   Maryanne!

Maryanne   – it must surely be some miracle.

Lieut Coyle   For God's sake, can't you keep your mouth shut for five minutes?!

The door bursts open; the bed that is propped up against it falls.

Lieut Ryan *enters, dragging a slaughtered pig tied to a rope.*

Lieut Ryan   Dead pig, sir.

Lieut Coyle   What?!

Lieut Ryan   Dead pig.

Lieut Coyle   I can see what it is!

Maryanne (*to* **Ellen**)   Come here, darling, come here.

Ellen *scrambles over to* **Maryanne**.

Over the following, **Maryanne** *spits on her sleeve and cleans* **Ellen**'s *face, head and hands with it.*

Lieut Coyle (*to* **Ryan**)   Jesus Christ, Ryan, you don't have to drag it around like an old bagpipe!

Lieut Ryan   But, sir, I didn't know what else to —

Lieut Coyle   Where was it?

Lieut Ryan   What?

Lieut Coyle   Where did you find it?

Lieut Ryan   Oh . . .

Lieut Coyle   Won't you speak?

Lieut Ryan   Oh, yes, sir.

Lieut Coyle   I suppose it just slipped out your arse, did it?

Lieut Ryan   No, I found it on the pass just now, sir, I think . . .

Lieut Coyle   You think.

Lieut Ryan   Sir, please, it wasn't there before.

Lieut Coyle   Did you see anyone?

Lieut Ryan   It's still breathing, look.

Lieut Coyle   When I ask a question, Lieutenant . . .

Lieut Ryan   If you would just let me answer . . .

Lieut Coyle   Was there a trail?

Pause.

Lieut Ryan   Sir, please . . .

Lieut Coyle   Were there footprints?

Lieut Ryan *hesitates.*

Lieut Coyle   Were there footprints, Lieutenant? Speak!

Lieut Ryan   I don't remember.

Lieut Coyle   What?

Lieut Ryan   I don't recall.

Lieut Coyle   Did you even look?

Lieut Ryan *hesitates.*

Lieut Coyle   For God's sake, man!

Lieut Ryan   Sir, please, you can't –

Lieut Coyle   You must have seen something!

Lieut Ryan   Lower your voice.

Lieut Coyle   What?

Lieut Ryan   Lower your voice, sir, you can't speak to me like that.

Lieut Coyle   Are you trying to – ?

Lieut Ryan   You can't speak to me like a common –

Lieut Coyle *hits* **Lieut Ryan** *across the head.*

Lieut Ryan   Aah!

Lieut Coyle *grabs* **Lieut Ryan** *and drags him aside.*

Lieut Coyle   I'll speak to you as I choose.

Lieut Ryan   No, please . . .

Lieut Coyle   Threaten me in front of these fucking peasants, have you lost your senses, boy? Can't you see what we're up against?

Lieut Ryan   I can see with my own two eyes –

Lieut Coyle   You see what I bid thee, Ryan, and nothing more. Don't think for one moment that there's any truth in what this woman claims. (*Laughs.*) That I would in any way be bound to a Catholic!

Lieut Ryan   Well, are you, sir?

Lieut Coyle *strikes* **Lieut Ryan**.

Lieut Ryan   Aah!

Lieut Coyle   That is treason, Lieutenant!

Lieut Ryan   Sir, please, you can't –

Lieut Coyle   What, am I your ensign?

He strikes **Lieut Ryan**.

Lieut Ryan   Aah!

Lieut Coyle   Come at me with your poison! For how long have we been sworn?

Lieut Ryan   But, sir –

Lieut Coyle   For how long, Lieutenant Ryan?

Lieut Ryan   Please, I'll tell my uncle!

Lieut Coyle   You'll what?

Lieut Ryan   I'll tell my uncle, sir, please, you can't speak to me like this!

Lieut Coyle   Are you my second or aren't you?

Lieut Ryan   My family own two-fifths of this land. I will not be treated like a common soldier.

Lieut Coyle   Your family saw fit to put you under my command, Ryan.

Lieut Ryan   But it is –

Lieut Coyle   That was their wish.

Lieut Ryan   It is improper, sir, please!

Lieut Coyle   Are you my second, boy? – Answer!

Lieut Ryan   Of course, sir, just –

Lieut Coyle   Then you will do as you are bid, you will learn by example.

Lieut Ryan   Example!

Lieut Coyle   The example of my stripes, you belligerent seed, you sapling. What? Do they frighten you?

Lieut Ryan   Frighten me?

Lieut Coyle   Do the spirits of the forest frighten you, Lieutenant? The ghosts and foul demons that wait among the trees? Why, they'll set a man against his wits if he dares not stand firm. Are you to be held to ransom by a pagan's superstition?

Lieut Ryan   No, I mean –

Lieut Coyle   Or will it be Luther you follow? Oh, come on, Lieutenant, you're shaking in your boots, look.

Lieut Ryan   I mean, yes, sir, of course, quite right!

Lieut Coyle   Well, don't just stand there, fool!

Lieut Ryan   Sir!

Lieut Coyle   Find out who did this! Go on with you!

Lieut Ryan *exits.*

Lieut Coyle   Jesus save us all . . .

Ellen   Is Daddy not well?

Maryanne   Oh no, child.

Lieut Coyle (*at the pig*)   Are you out of your fucking mind?!

Maryanne   No, it's just the excitement of Easter, he'll soon calm down.

Lieut Coyle (*takes his dagger*)   Pity the poor swine!

Maryanne   Isn't that so, Lieutenant?

Lieut Coyle   Jabbing at its brain like he was trying to free its very conscience. Did you not train him how to use a knife?

Maryanne   That's your duty.

Lieut Coyle   Could he not have shown a little mercy at least?!

Maryanne   Lieutenant . . .

Lieut Coyle   This is how you kill a pig!

Lieut Coyle *cuts the pig's throat. The pig squeals.*

Squatting over the dead pig, **Lieut Coyle** *catches his breath.*

The storm continues.

Long pause.

Ellen   Should I sing the song now, Mammy?

Long pause.

Mammy.

Maryanne   Oh, that would be lovely, darling.

Ellen (*to* **Coyle**)   Mammy taught me a hymn.

Lieut Coyle (*to* **Maryanne**)   You sent him, didn't you?

Ellen   Would you like to hear it?

Pause.

Ellen   Daddy . . .

Lieut Coyle (*to* **Maryanne**)   You sent him.

Ellen   Daddy, please . . .

Lieut Coyle   It was you, Maryanne, you did this!

Maryanne (*to* **Ellen**)   Go and get into place now.

Lieut Coyle   If you think –

Maryanne (*to* **Ellen**)   Go on, child.

Lieut Coyle   If you expect me to stand before the Colonel and defend him –

Maryanne (*to* **Ellen**)   By the fire, remember?

Lieut Coyle   Maryanne!

Maryanne   Let her sing you her song, you old bastard, she's been waiting for you all day.

Pause.

Ellen *moves and stands by the peat fire.*

Lieut Coyle   Maryanne, please, you must –

Maryanne (*to* **Ellen**)   Take a deep breath now, go on.

Lieut Coyle   You must know that I can't –

Maryanne   Sit down, Lieutenant!

Lieut Coyle   I can't just relinquish my own company for the sake –

Maryanne   For the sake of your daughter! Well?!

Lieut Coyle *hesitates, then slams the cabin door shut and sits on the edge of the makeshift bed.*

Long pause.

Ellen (*sings*)
   Oh Paddy dear, and did you hear the news that's going
      round?
   The shamrock is by law unfit to grow on Irish ground,   *
   No more St Patrick's Day we'll keep, his colour can't be seen,
   For there's a cruel law against . . .

Maryanne/Ellen (*sing*)
   . . . the wearing of the green!

Maryanne *applauds* **Ellen**.

Maryanne   Oh, well, isn't she the angel!

Maryanne *motions for* **Lieut Coyle** *to applaud.*

Maryanne   Hasn't she the prettiest little voice! Hasn't she
though? Oh!

Lieut Coyle *applauds.* **Maryanne** *lifts up* **Ellen** *and kisses her.*

Maryanne   That was wonderful, darling!

Ellen   Thank you, Mammy.

Maryanne   Take a bow now, come on.

Ellen *bows.*

Maryanne (*applauds*)   Oh, look at her!

Ellen   Was that all right, Daddy?

Lieut Coyle   Yes . . .

Ellen   Could you hear every word?

Maryanne   We could hear the parchment it was set upon, my
love.

Ellen   Daddy . . .

Lieut Coyle   Yes, it was lovely, darling.

Maryanne (*to* **Ellen**)   You see, what did I tell you?

Lieut Coyle   Thank you.

Maryanne (*to* **Ellen**)   I told you he'd be pleased, didn't I?

Ellen   Would you like me to teach it?

Lieut Coyle   Oh . . . Oh, well . . .

Ellen   We could sing it together.

Lieut Coyle   Well, I don't think . . .

Ellen   That's right though, isn't it, Mammy?

Lieut Coyle   Maybe some other time.

Maryanne   Oh, don't be such a stuffed bull, Lieutenant . . .

Ellen   Daddy, please . . .

Lieut Coyle (*to* **Maryanne**)   I think you'd better . . .

Maryanne   . . . let her teach you her song, come on.

Ellen (*to* **Coyle**)   We could sing a line each then, couldn't we?

Lieut Coyle   Maybe some other time, Ellen.

Ellen   We could sing it on the boat.

Maryanne   Now that's a clever idea!

Ellen   We could sing it as we leave port.

Maryanne   That's right.

Ellen   We could . . .

Maryanne   We could sing it on the boat, couldn't we, Lieutenant?

Long pause.

Lieut Coyle   What?

Maryanne   Couldn't we just!

Lieut Coyle   What boat?

Maryanne   Have you not heard?

Ellen   The boat sailing for England.

Maryanne   That's right, Ellen, we saw it from the top field, didn't we? Why, you can almost hear it – listen. The wind on the sails. The rattle of the cannon upon the salted Shannon air.

Ellen   Mammy says there'll be angels waiting for us.

Maryanne   On the deck, Ellen, that's right. On the deck and in the crow's nest, a whole regiment of angels. Surely you've heard, Lieutenant?

Ellen   The Angel Gabriel.

Maryanne   You saw him in a dream, didn't you, girl?

Ellen   He steered the ship himself.

Lieut Coyle   Did he now?

Maryanne   Tell him about the mountains. You remember the snowy mountains, don't you, Ellen?

Ellen   Oh . . .

Maryanne   Reaching up through the clouds.

Lieut Coyle   Let her finish.

Ellen   Yes, Mammy, I do.

Maryanne   They do be lining the coast from Argyll to Land's End.

Ellen (*to* **Coyle**)   And we can see them in the distance.

Maryanne   They're in the distance and as we drop anchor . . .

Pause.

Maryanne   And as we drop anchor – come on now, girl, you remember.

Ellen   I don't . . .

Maryanne   You remember the Virgin Mary.

Ellen   Oh . . . Oh, yes.

Maryanne (*to* **Coyle**)   She'll forget her own mind.

Ellen   That's right, Mammy.

Maryanne   Waiting in her carriage to lead us safely home.

Ellen   To Buckingham Palace.

Maryanne (*to* **Coyle**)   It's so easy to forget in all this excitement.

Lieut Coyle   Quite.

Ellen   Mammy says I'll have my own maid.

Maryanne   You can have anything you want, my girl.

Ellen   Will I not have to bathe in the river any more?

Maryanne   We will be bathed in milk.

Ellen   Will we not have to work until nightfall?

Maryanne (*laughs*)   Work! What work?! The work of a fat old Persian cat, I grant you!

Ellen   Might we have our own roof? A roof with real wooden walls?

Maryanne   Well, if we pray very hard . . .

Ellen   Might I have a bed of my own?

Maryanne   You might want to ask your . . .

Ellen   Daddy.

Pause.

Ellen   Daddy . . .

Lieut Coyle   No.

Ellen   Will brother Dermot be with us?

Long pause.

Daddy . . .

Lieut Coyle (*to* **Maryanne**)   That's no hymn for a child.

Ellen   Have I said something wrong?

Pause.

Lieut Coyle   Of course not, darling.

Ellen   Did I speak the wrong line?

Maryanne   Now come on, Ellen, don't be tiring out your father.

Ellen   But I only –

Maryanne   Travelling all that way from town – (*To* **Coyle**.) I'm surprised you're not flat on your back, Lieutenant.

Lieut Coyle   Now don't you –

Maryanne (*to* **Ellen**)   I'm surprised he's not face down in a puddle!

Lieut Coyle   Don't push me, Maryanne.

Maryanne   How you'll fare against the French is a mystery to me.

Lieut Coyle   What?

Maryanne   The French, sir.

Lieut Coyle   Now, listen –

Maryanne   How you'll manage in battle – by my foot, I can only pray you've got the blessing of King George. Though I do hear you'll be flanked by the Prussian Army at least.

Lieut Coyle   Who told you?

Maryanne   And whose banner will you bear, I wonder?

Lieut Coyle   Maryanne . . .

Maryanne   The red, white and blue?

Lieut Coyle   I'm not –

Maryanne   The green perhaps?

Lieut Coyle   I'm not playing your –

Maryanne   The orange!

Will it be the orange, Lieutenant?

Pause.

Lieutenant . . .

Lieut Coyle   Who told you?

Who was it?

Maryanne   We will pray for you, of course. In the Abbey.

Lieut Coyle   What?

Maryanne   Westminster Abbey. (*To* **Ellen**.) We'll ask the Pope for salvation, won't we, child?

Ellen   Yes, Mammy.

Maryanne   We'll call on Jesus to bring the enemy to his knees.

Ellen   Oh, yes, that's right . . .

Maryanne   To see him safely home.

Ellen   To the Palace.

Maryanne   To the light and love of Old England.

Well?

What do you think, Lieutenant? Is it a good plan?

Long pause.

Thomas . . .

Lieut Coyle   You want to watch what you say.

Maryanne   Now don't disappoint the poor girl.

Lieut Coyle   You should be mindful what you teach.

Maryanne   Go on, Ellen, the token.

Ellen   I kept a token for you, look.

She removes a chain that is fastened round her neck. On it hangs a crucifix.

Look, Daddy.

She offers the chain/crucifix to **Lieut Coyle**.

Ellen   To protect you, look.

Pause.

You can wear it round your neck.

Lieut Coyle   Yes, that's . . .

Ellen   To remind you that I'll always be with you. Won't you take it?

Pause.

Daddy . . .

Lieut Coyle   Run along now.

Ellen   Don't you like it?

Lieut Coyle   Run along, go on.

Ellen   But . . .

Lieut Coyle   Go and say your prayers, there's a good girl.

Ellen   But I saved it . . .

Lieut Coyle   It's way past your bedtime, Ellen, that's enough.

Ellen   But I saved it for you.

Lieut Coyle   Go on now.

Ellen   Daddy, look, I –

Lieut Coyle   Go on!

Lieut Coyle *snatches the chain/crucifix from* **Ellen**.

Ellen   Daddy, please!

Maryanne   Answer the girl.

Lieut Coyle (*to* **Maryanne**)   You know they'll drown you in the river just for having this alone!

Maryanne   Oh, come now, Lieutenant, she only meant –

Lieut Coyle   She meant nothing, Maryanne!

Ellen   You can keep my missal.

Lieut Coyle   What?

Ellen   My missal.

She takes a missal from her pocket, offering it to **Lieut Coyle**.

Ellen   My prayer book, Daddy, you can read it on the battlefield.

Lieut Coyle   Jesus Christ . . .

Ellen   You can call on the saints to protect you –

Lieut Coyle (*snatches the missal*)   That's an order, child!

Ellen   To protect you from all evil –

Lieut Coyle   Wait outside, for the love of God! For the love of God –

He whisks **Ellen** *out of the cabin door, shutting it up behind her.*

Lieut Coyle   – that you should have ever been born, wait outside, I say!

Maryanne   Will your wife be joining you?

Lieut Coyle   What?

Maryanne   You heard me.

Long pause.

She moves to the peat fire, and removes the pot from the fire. She ladles the potato stew from out of the pot and into a small bowl.

Will your wife be joining you, Lieutenant?

Lieut Coyle   Look . . .

Maryanne   The anticipation must be almost too much to bear. A woman of her years.

Lieut Coyle   All right . . .

Maryanne   A woman of her size. Have they cleared an extra deck for her, Lieutenant?

Lieut Coyle   You leave her out of this.

Maryanne   She has her own galleon, no? I imagine her family could afford a whole fleet if they so pleased.

Maryanne   Coming from such Cromwellian stock.

Lieut Coyle   That's enough.

Maryanne   Is she a saint, I wonder?

Lieut Coyle   Maryanne . . .

Maryanne   To marry a poor peasant like you.

Lieut Coyle   Don't . . .

Maryanne   That's some act of charity!

Long pause.

That is charity indeed.

Pause.

She must think she has you trained like one of her miserable pooches.

Lieut Coyle   All right . . .

Maryanne   She'll have you auctioned the moment you reach shore.

Lieut Coyle   Maryanne . . .

Maryanne   A symbol of the Commonwealth no less. A trophy of their good works.

Lieut Coyle   She's a good woman.

Maryanne   Is she joining you?

Lieut Coyle   She's more virtue than you'll ever know.

Maryanne   Your horse?

Lieut Coyle   What?

Maryanne   Are you taking your horse?

Pause.

Are you taking your horse, sir?

Lieut Coyle   Maryanne . . .

Maryanne   Crawl away.

Lieut Coyle   What?

Maryanne   Break the girl's heart.

Long pause.

Lieut Coyle   She's a sweetheart.

Maryanne   She's right.

Lieut Coyle   She needs protecting, she doesn't –

Maryanne   She's a vision of fucking purity, any fool can see that.

Lieut Coyle   She doesn't deserve to have her mind played tricks with.

Maryanne   Did you think you could just creep away?

Lieut Coyle   It's up to you to protect her, Maryanne.

Maryanne   Do you not care about your daughter?

Lieut Coyle   Of course I care!

Maryanne   Does it not matter if she rots?

Lieut Coyle   I don't have any choice, woman!

Maryanne   Oh, I see.

Lieut Coyle   A man must have reason, he must have order.

Maryanne   Oh, well . . .

Lieut Coyle   Regardless of faith! There must be political order, Maryanne.

Maryanne   Well, since you put it that way, sir.

Lieut Coyle   Believe me . . .

Maryanne   I am enlightened.

Lieut Coyle   Believe me, if I could place you in the squadron I would. If I could plant a beard on your chin and teach you how to use a sword. If by holy conversion alone you might be saved from this poverty, and if –

Maryanne   If I were an oaf like you.

Lieut Coyle   Is this the suit of an oaf? Is this colour and purse . . . ?

Maryanne   You're nothing but a farmer, Coyle.

Lieut Coyle   What?

Maryanne   You're a trained monkey, that's all.

Lieut Coyle   For Christ's sake . . .

Maryanne   Stand aside while your own family starves.

Lieut Coyle   You can't seriously expect me to hide in a quarry like the rest of you fucking animals.

Maryanne   Oh, animals now, is it?

Lieut Coyle   Well, can you?!

Maryanne   Oh no, sir.

Lieut Coyle   Maryanne . . .

Maryanne   An animal would never betray his own kind.

Lieut Coyle   Have I not kept you in food and water for the past God knows how many years? Have I not lent you money and clothes? When my brother died, I swore that I'd take care of you.

Maryanne   Oh, you took care of me all right.

Lieut Coyle   That's right, woman, I kept my promise, no matter whose side we're on. Do you think you would even be here if I hadn't took the oath? I gave you children, for God's sake, what more proof do you need?! When they moved you off the farm, did I not leave you with the little they would have otherwise burnt? They would have thrown you all on the fire had I not pleaded with them. Had I not begged and threatened my own standing, and for what?! For you to set that madman loose and to blackmail me with your own daughter?

Maryanne   She's your daughter too.

Lieut Coyle   Is this what you teach her?

Maryanne   Teach her, Lieutenant?

Lieut Coyle   You're out to punish me!

Maryanne   Oh no, sir, I know my rights.

Lieut Coyle   Maryanne . . .

Maryanne   I've spent a lifetime under Penal Law, I know my place.

Lieut Coyle   If you think for one moment –

Maryanne   The Catholic does not trespass upon occupied land, Lieutenant. The Catholic does not trade, rent, lease and he surely does not steal from the property of his betters, let alone butcher the swine that keeps it.

Lieut Coyle   Oh, then forgive me my fucking . . .

Maryanne   There's no doubt to be found in me, sir.

Lieut Coyle   No doubt!

Maryanne   The Catholic does not exercise his religion, neither will he receive education. He will not enter a profession, nor will he hold public office. He will not buy or lease any land, and God forbid that he should vote. – Would you like me to go on? The Catholic will not bear Catholic children, and he shall be fined should he not attend the Protestant church. He shall not carry gun, pistol or sword under penalty of fine, pillory or public whipping. He will be fined and executed should he own a horse for over the alloted sum – that's five pounds to you and me, Lieutenant, we all remember that. He will not own a horse, nor will he receive a gift or inheritance from any man, least of all the Protestant. He shall serve the Protestant at his command, but he shall not live within five miles of one. He shall not live near town nor village nor shit upon the soil unless he wish to kiss the hangman. He shall not live at all, sir. No, I am indeed schooled in that solemn verse, I know where my allegiance lies.

Lieut Coyle   Your allegiance lies to no one, filth.

Maryanne   This same filth bore you children, Lieutenant. Do you think I would dare jeopardise the only thing I have left?

Lieut Coyle   I know what I see before me.

Maryanne   The Treaty of Limerick was passed some hundred years ago, Lieutenant. I've had a lifetime and beyond to know my rights. If your brother had not betrayed the law of English, had he not had your strength . . .

Lieut Coyle   Don't you breathe a word about that man.

Maryanne   He was my husband, Thomas!

Lieut Coyle   I've told you before –

Maryanne   Had he not been too weak to play your dirty game and keep up this pretence –

Lieut Coyle   That's enough!

Maryanne   We would be living on that farm to this day, Thomas – do you think I don't know that?

Lieut Coyle   All right –

Maryanne   The rebellion died at the sword of Oliver Cromwell, do you think I would sacrifice this poor girl's soul for that – for what? For the will and charity of the Roman Catholic Church?

Lieut Coyle   No, of course not.

Maryanne   Should I send her to the gallows for that hollow cause?

Lieut Coyle   Look . . .

Maryanne   Should I do that, Thomas?

Lieut Coyle   If they were to find her with this –

He pulls out the chain/crucifix.

– Catholic filth, it is forbidden! What, should I brand it on her fucking hide?!

Maryanne   You can't deny the girl her faith, sir.

Lieut Coyle   Do you want her to grow into her brother? Is that what you want?

Maryanne   The boy's madness is your doing.

Lieut Coyle   I can only pray he hasn't corrupted her already.

Maryanne   Well, if you were ever home to protect the poor thing.

Lieut Coyle   What?

Maryanne   If you were ever home . . .

Lieut Coyle   We're at war, for Christ's sake!

Maryanne   And whose war is that, sir?

Lieut Coyle   Oh, come on, Maryanne . . .

Maryanne   You overfed eunuch.

Lieut Coyle   If you would just stop . . .

Maryanne   You Negro.

Lieut Coyle   Stop . . .

Maryanne   You piss-grovelling growth on the cock-end of the Commonwealth.

Long pause.

Have I said something to offend you?

Pause.

Lieutenant.

Lieut Coyle   Hold out your hand.

Maryanne   What?

Lieut Coyle   Your hand.

He puts the crucifix back in his pocket, and, at the same time, removes his purse.

Pause.

Give me your hand.

Maryanne   Oh . . .

Lieut Coyle   For the girl.

Maryanne   That's very thoughtful of you, sir.

Lieut Coyle *empties his purse onto* **Maryanne**'s *hand.*

Lieut Coyle   Three guineas.

Maryanne   Well, I . . .

Lieut Coyle   Keep it.

Maryanne   I'm lost for words, Lieutenant.

Lieut Coyle   Are you going to tell me where he is?

Maryanne   Three guineas.

Lieut Coyle   The boy.

Maryanne   For an old papist whore.

Lieut Coyle   Tell me.

Maryanne (*counting the coins*)   You might purge the living Devil with this.

Lieut Coyle   Where might I find him?

Pause.

Maryanne, come on now . . .

Maryanne   And will you grant her liberty?

Lieut Coyle   What?

Maryanne   Will you grant the girl her freedom, sir?

Lieut Coyle   Look . . .

Maryanne   Will you do that?

Lieut Coyle   Woman, please, I have never –

Maryanne   There must be some space on that boat of yours.

Lieut Coyle   I have never promised –

Maryanne   There must be somewhere we could hide.

Lieut Coyle   In all our time together –

Maryanne   In the name of Jesus, will you not find some way for your own flesh and blood?

Lieut Coyle   You can't expect me –

Maryanne   Will you not consider it, even?

Lieut Coyle   Maryanne –

Maryanne   Will you do that for me, even?

Lieut Coyle   Maryanne, please –

Maryanne   Will you do that, Thomas? – Answer me!

Long pause.

Lieut Coyle   Maryanne . . .

Maryanne   Then you would forget the love we shared . . .

Lieut Coyle   What?

Maryanne   Then you would deny all tenderness, no?

Long pause.

Lieut Coyle   Maryanne, please.

Pause.

He touches **Maryanne** *tenderly by her shoulders.*

Lieut Coyle   Please, you know if there was any other way . . .

Maryanne   Of course she would make a beautiful young bride.

Lieut Coyle   What?

Maryanne   She would make a fine bride, sir.

Pause.

Lieut Coyle   What?

Maryanne   One of your honest English captains, I should imagine.

Lieut Coyle   Now look . . .

Maryanne   One of your kin.

Lieut Coyle   I'm warning you . . .

Maryanne   Three guineas, he says.

Lieut Coyle   Don't . . .

Maryanne   I could trade three sheep off her virginity alone.

Lieut Coyle *grabs* **Maryanne** *by the hair.*

Maryanne   Now that's what we call a wager, sir.

Long pause.

Lieut Coyle   Is she on the rag?

Pause.

Maryanne . . .

Maryanne   What?

Lieut Coyle   Is she on the rag?

Maryanne   Pull it out with your teeth.

Lieut Coyle *draws his sword with his free hand.*

Lieut Coyle   Living Devil, you!

Maryanne   And may you choke on it, sir.

Lieut Coyle   I should cut your filthy tongue out!

Maryanne   Do you want me to scream?

Lieut Coyle *aims his sword at* **Maryanne**'s *face.*

Lieut Coyle   Tell me where he is, damn you!

Maryanne   You want me to scream, Lieutenant?

Lieut Coyle   That's enough of your treachery!

Maryanne   You want me to fall on my knees?

Lieut Coyle   For the last time . . . !

Maryanne   I'll tell you nothing.

Lieut Coyle   Hand him over to me – speak!

Maryanne   Unless it's my blood you're after . . .

Lieut Coyle   Your blood is right, woman.

Maryanne   Well, go on!

Ellen (*off*)   Mammy!

Maryanne   Go on, I said!

Ellen *quickly enters, pursued by* **Lieut Ryan**.

Ellen (*as she enters*)   Mammy, please, I was only trying to climb the horse!

Lieut Coyle   Answer me!

Ellen   Tell him, Mammy, tell him!

Maryanne   I'll not make a squeak, you mongrel.

Ellen   He thinks I was trying to steal it, but I wasn't, I swear!

Lieut Coyle   To Hell with you!

He slashes **Maryanne**'*s face.*

Ellen   Mammy!

Lieut Coyle *pushes* **Maryanne** *off her stool.*

Ellen   Mammy, no!

Blackout.

Three

The tavern.

Night.

The storm continues outside.

Dermot *and* **Sgt Browne**, **Capt Farrell**, **Capt Skelton**, *and* **Cpl O'Connor** *are sitting at a table, with drinks.* **Dermot** *is covered in blood, and clutching onto a dead piglet. With his other hand he wields a blunt knife. Attached to his ankles are chains that should be fastened together and then tied to a tree, but are unlocked, allowing him to move freely.*

L-Cpl Finnigan *guards the tavern door. The* **Pot-Boy** *is serving drinks. The* **Fiddler** *and the* **Piper** *play music in the corner.*

On the wall hangs a large portrait of King George III among angels, as he ascends to Heaven.

Dermot   . . . and there's just him and me and we're down on the ground and I have the little bastard by the throat. He's wriggling and squealing like the very plague pins him down. 'No more!' he cries. 'Have mercy!'

The **Redcoats** *laugh.*

Dermot   'Spare a penny for my soul!'

Sgt Browne (*laughing*)   Pour the boy a drink!

Dermot   Boxing my head with his four trotters he was! Lashing his tongue as if his spit would burn my very flesh – I tell you, this was no ordinary pig!

Capt Farrell   God save us!

Dermot   I swear he might have crushed my very skull had he the property! Had I not the will of Jesus Christ at my hand, had I not lived to taste the sacrament!

Capt Skelton   Pity the poor beast.

Dermot   Of course I finished him.

Cpl O'Connor   You slashed him?

Dermot   I cut his very heart out!

Cpl O'Connor   From ear to ear?

Dermot   From top to stinking toe.

Capt Farrell   I don't believe it.

Dermot   As God is my witness . . .

Capt Skelton   As God is your what?

Capt Farrell   The boy couldn't crack an egg without crying to his mammy!

They laugh.

Dermot   I have him gaping like an old drunken whore, I do!

Sgt Browne (*to the* **Pot-Boy**)   Are you deaf, you fucking weasel?

Dermot (*to* **O'Connor**)   I have him begging for mercy, I tell you.

Cpl O'Connor   Do you now?

Dermot   I have him dragging his four legs through the mud and through the marshes. Of course I can barely see my own rotten body never mind the remains of this poor beast. But I keep him gripped. I keep him gripped against my hips like he's a Sheela-na-Gig, by Christ, as your very skin might hold its wound! The thunder's cracking skulls and the lightning clips my heels, but I charge and I charge till we're lost within the Vale. It's here we catch our breath and with him beating at my face, I slit him like a medlar and he tumbles to his death!

The **Redcoats** *laugh and clap.* **Sgt Browne** *kisses* **Dermot**.

Sgt Browne (*laughing*)   Give me a kiss, me boy!

Dermot   That'll teach him, won't it?

Sgt Browne (*laughing*)   Papist scum, you!

Capt Farrell (*laughing*)   You filthy bastard, Sergeant Browne!

Dermot   That'll teach him, look!

Capt Farrell   You'll bring us all down with the plague!

Sgt Browne   Fill up his beaker, damn you!

Dermot (*to* **O'Connor**)   Tell me that'll teach him though, won't it?

Cpl O'Connor (*laughing*)   Oh, it's a fine story, I'll grant you.

Sgt Browne   Fine story!

Cpl O'Connor   It does well raise a few eyebrows, Sergeant Browne.

Sgt Browne   This is the stuff of kings, my lad!

Dermot   It is?

Sgt Browne   You'll be decorated for this, I grant you!

Capt Farrell   Did he offend you?

Dermot   What?

Capt Skelton   This beast you speak of.

Capt Farrell   You must have good reason.

Cpl O'Connor   Let's pray he was no Prussian.

Capt Skelton   What had he done to you exactly?

Dermot   Done?

Capt Farrell   His crime, boy, his crime!

Cpl O'Connor   You must have killed for a reason, lad, come on.

Dermot   But I just told –

Capt Farrell (*mimics* **Dermot**)   Sodomy, by God!

They laugh.

Capt Farrell (*mimics* **Dermot**, *raising his glass*)   In the name of Our Grace!

Sgt Browne   In the name of the Pontiff!

Capt Skelton   Did he stain your noble honour?

Capt Farrell/Sgt Browne   In the name of the Pope!

More laughter – they toast and drink, filling their beakers from the **Pot-Boy**'s *jug.*

Cpl O'Connor   Get it down you, lad, get it down!

Dermot   But I don't know what you mean . . .

Sgt Browne   Finish your drink, you cold-hearted bastard!

Dermot   On my honour –

Capt Skelton   His honour – now did I not tell you?

Dermot   By the honour of the Virgin Mary —

Capt Skelton   The boy's a martyr, by Christ!

Cpl O'Connor   Was it justice you were seeking?

Dermot   What?

Sgt Browne   Should we send for the bailiffs, young sir?

Capt Farrell   Should we keep watch for when he returns?

Dermot   When who returns?

Sgt Browne (*calls*)   Send for the watch!

Dermot   No, you're not hearing me.

Sgt Browne   The watch!

Dermot   You're not hearing me, please!

Sgt Browne (*calls to the* **Pot-Boy**)   Send for the watch, lad!

Capt Farrell   There's a door here lost its hinges!

Sgt Browne   Send for the watch, I say!

Dermot   But you're not hearing me out, boys!

Cpl O'Connor   Oh, we hear you, Dermot, we hear you.

Capt Skelton   Ah, but can we trust his word?

Dermot   I tell you, I killed him!

Capt Farrell/Sgt Browne   Oh!

Dermot   I tore his stinking apple out! With me own front teeth!

Cpl O'Connor   All right, we hear you, Dermot!

Dermot   Why do you think I braved the storm?!

Capt Farrell   So you might hang off my balls?

Dermot   Why would I do that?

Cpl O'Connor   Oh, you can be sure we'll find good reason.

Dermot   I tell you, I never saw such suffering as in this foul pig!

As **Dermot** *speaks, the* **Redcoats** *fill up their drinks.*

Capt Farrell *takes* **Dermot***'s cup and pisses in it. The cup is then passed to each* **Redcoat***, each man spitting in it.*

Dermot   He wept and he prayed, but I wouldn't grant him penance – no, I wouldn't be his witness. They can all of them rot in Hell before I'll hand him back to Jesus, if they think I'll toss forgiveness like a beggar to a fool. The animal's mine, by God, and I'd sooner sell the Temple! I'd sooner trade the Baptist than to toil another day. To have her use me for a haywain, to have her curse me like a mule – and for what?

Capt Farrell/Sgt Browne   'For what?'

Dermot   To keep me from my liberty, to keep me from the call. To keep me from my duty, that to serve you, one and all!

The **Redcoats** *laugh.*

Dermot   It's true, I tell you!

Cpl O'Connor (*laughing*)   A soldier no less!

Capt Farrell (*laughing*)   To honour and to serve . . .

Capt Skelton (*laughing*)   Amen!

Sgt Browne (*laughing*)   Amen is right!

Cpl O'Connor (*laughing*)   Why didn't you tell us before, boy?

Sgt Browne (*laughing*)   Amen if he were to ever join my regiment!

Dermot   Let me join you, masters, please!

Capt Farrell (*laughing*)   Shall we recruit him, do you think?

Sgt Browne   On your life, Captain Farrell.

Dermot   You think I'm mad?!

Sgt Browne (*to* **Farrell**)   I'd sooner employ your bedwetting ma.

Dermot   You think I don't know?!

Capt Farrell   I think you'd better calm down.

Dermot   You think I haven't seen them?!

Capt Farrell   Now, come on, Dermot . . .

Dermot   You think I haven't seen the ships?!

Capt Skelton   Get a hold on yourself!

Dermot   You think I haven't seen them? You think I don't know what you're plotting? To keep me from my freedom, to keep me stranded on this isle. Chained like a prisoner while you sail away with Daddy – do you think I don't know?

Cpl O'Connor   Oh, we know all right.

Dermot   She told me herself, she did.

Cpl O'Connor   Oh, she did. God bless her.

Dermot   It came from her own two lips, the witch!

Sgt Browne   A witch, he claims!

Dermot   The witch my mother – don't you laugh at me!

Capt Farrell   Who's laughing?

Dermot   She'd lay a curse on you in a second!

Capt Farrell   Do you see me laughing, Captain Skelton?

Dermot   Mother of mine with her four fiendish heads! A monster, I grant you, a malignant maternal moan!

Capt Farrell   She has how many heads?

Dermot   Aye, and a fifth growing out from her hunchback!

Capt Farrell   It would seem she needs a surgeon, my lad.

Dermot   There's not a surgeon could contend with her foul humours, she's a witch and nothing more! – Don't laugh, I say, she'll have you in the mouth of Hell if you do so dare mock!

Capt Farrell (*laughs*)   Oh!

Capt Skelton   Are you threatening us, Dermot?

Dermot   I've had a lifetime bent under her inhuman will. If you could see what I have had to suffer! Chained and beat like a flea-bitten rover, as though I were two balls short of a man. Kept as a slave as though I were no better than a black man! A foreigner who couldn't claim a sword if it struck him, nor to even dream of being one of you proud gentlemen, and to honour and to serve his country.

Capt Skelton   Whose country?

Dermot   Any but this.

Capt Skelton   A traitor no less!

Dermot   Why do you think I came and sought you out?!

Capt Skelton   A traitor to his own fair land!

Dermot   She dragged me out of the cabin she did, out of my own home! She told me to come and find you, that I myself might beg your service! 'Go and prove yourself a killer, Dermot, go and find your precious daddy! Go and tell them you want to live the life of a soldier, boy, for I'm done with you!'

Cpl O'Connor   Oh, she didn't!

Dermot   Her own son disowned!

Cpl O'Connor   This is a sorry tale.

Dermot   That I should ever call her mother of mine!

Cpl O'Connor   Let it out, son, let it out.

Dermot   She wants to see me fail, I tell you! She wants to keep him for herself and to leave me at the mercy of the storm! If you would only help me prove her wrong, if you might see my potential.

Cpl O'Connor (*to* **Browne**)   I once saw a witch in the forest, by God.

Dermot   I slaughtered them for you, look!

Sgt Browne   It's a trick, I tell you!

Dermot   But I did it all for you!

Capt Skelton   Now now, Dermot . . .

Dermot   To prove that I can kill, to prove to my daddy!

Sgt Browne   Finish your drink now, sit down.

Cpl O'Connor   You've hardly wet your lip, look.

Capt Skelton *throws his drink at* **Dermot**'s *face.*

Capt Skelton   Call yourself a man, finish your drink!

Dermot   But I can't –

Cpl O'Connor   Go on, boy!

Dermot   But you can't expect me to –

Capt Farrell   Go on, you worm!

Capt Farrell *forces the cup of piss and spit down* **Dermot**'s *throat.*

Capt Skelton   Loosen your tongue!

Farrell/O'Connor/Skelton   Drink it up! / Go on, Dermot! / Every last drop, go on! (*Etc.*)

Sgt Browne (*to the* **Pot-Boy**)   Are you going to just stand there, lad?

Sgt Browne *takes the piglet and throws it to the* **Pot-Boy**.

Sgt Browne   Tie it to the spit, go on!

The **Pot-Boy** *takes the piglet. During the following he ties it to the spit over the fire and roasts the piglet, slowly turning the spit.*

Sgt Browne (*to the* **Pot-Boy**)   That I must suffer this watered-down swill, do you want me to starve to death as well?!

The **Redcoats** *cheer as* **Dermot** *finishes his drink.*

Cpl O'Connor (*laughing*)   By Christ, you're a marvel, lad!

Sgt Browne   Marvel nothing, it's a plot!

Cpl O'Connor   But he's a killer, by God!

Sgt Browne   Killer my backside!

Cpl O'Connor   He was sent by his own dear mammy!

Sgt Browne   He couldn't hurt a bee if it stung him.

Dermot   I could cut you down to size!

Sgt Browne   Oh, really?

Dermot   I could take you down with my little finger if I be so pleased!

Sgt Browne   Is that a challenge, boy?

Dermot   I could claim you for a signet on my wedding day.

Sgt Browne (*to* **O'Connor**)   Is he challenging me, Corporal?

Dermot   Do I look like a coward to you?

Sgt Browne   Damn you to Hell!

Dermot (*strikes* **Browne**)   Well, do I?

The **Redcoats** *laugh.*

Capt Farrell (*laughs*)   Oh, he's no coward, Sergeant, I'll lay my life on that.

Dermot (*strikes* **Browne**)   Red-breasted oaf!

Sgt Browne   By Christ!

Dermot (*strikes* **Browne**)   I should use you for my –

Sgt Browne *grabs* **Dermot** *by the throat. The others laugh.*

Dermot   Aah!

Sgt Browne   Now, listen . . .

Dermot (*struggling for breath*)   Please . . .

Sgt Browne   Are you listening?

Dermot (*struggling, nods*)   I – I – I – I . . .

Again, over the dialogue, the **Redcoats** *fill up the cups with drink.*

Sgt Browne *has* **Dermot** *by the throat.*

Sgt Browne   Do you know who I am?

Dermot *struggles to speak.*

Sgt Browne   Do you see that portrait on the wall?

Dermot *struggles to speak.*

Sgt Browne   Do you not recognise your King?

Dermot *struggles to speak.*

Sgt Browne   Well, do you?

Dermot *struggles to speak.*

Sgt Browne   You think you can come here and lay claim to His Majesty's keepers? Am I no more than a pot-boy to you?

Capt Skelton   Let him go, Sergeant.

Sgt Browne   Am I and these fine fellows –

Capt Skelton   You'll break his neck you carry on.

Sgt Browne   – are we no better than the pigs you claim to fight on?

Cpl O'Connor   Come now, Sergeant Browne, don't –

Sgt Browne   Well?!

Sgt Browne *slams* **Dermot**'s *head on the table.*

Dermot (*gasping for breath*)   No!

Sgt Browne   Have you come to taunt us, soldier?

Dermot (*gasping*)   Please . . .

Sgt Browne   Have you come to taunt us?

Dermot (*gasping*)   Please, I beg you . . .

Sgt Browne   Come to taunt us on the eve of battle. The last night in our own fair country, the land that bore us.

Dermot (*gasping*)   I only want to –

Sgt Browne   Are we not allowed some celebration?

Dermot (*gasping*)   Of course, of course –

Sgt Browne   A time to grieve at least?

Dermot (*gasping*)   I deny you nothing, sir.

Sgt Browne   Can I not share a drink with these noble men for whom I'd wage my own life?

Dermot (*gasping*)   You can drink all you like!

Capt Skelton   Murdering swine, you.

Dermot   What?

Capt Skelton   Murdering cunt.

Dermot   But I only want –

Sgt Browne   Come to ruin our party.

Cpl O'Connor   We should gut the stinking wretch.

Dermot   But I only want to help!

Cpl O'Connor   I should toast his kidneys for me horse.

Sgt Browne   I'll toast to that!

Dermot   Let me fight your honourable cause!

Cpl O'Connor   Honourable cause.

Sgt Browne   I'll toast the kidneys, the horse and its mare, by Christ, my soul's already damned!

Capt Skelton   And whom should we fight, Dermot?

Dermot   The French!

Capt Farrell   Oh, the French!

Dermot   We fight the French, sir! We fight for the Commonwealth, we do! We fight for the wealth and rights of every living Englishman!

Capt Skelton   Do you bewitch us, Dermot?

Dermot   Bewitch? No, of course not!

Capt Farrell   On your feet.

Dermot   But it's true, boys, I swear my life on it!

Capt Farrell   On your feet, come on!

Capt Farrell *slams his sword on the table. The other* **Redcoats** *cheer.*

Capt Farrell   Give me your sword. O'Connor.

Sgt Browne   On your feet, you heard the man!

Dermot   But haven't I proved myself enough?

Sgt Browne/Cpl O'Connor   On your feet!

Dermot *is pulled to his feet by* **Sgt Browne** *and* **Cpl O'Connor.**

Sgt Browne   And so Lazarus arose.

Dermot   No . . .

Capt Farrell   At arms, boy!

Dermot   No, please, you're hurting me.

During the following **Capt Farrell** *takes* **Cpl O'Connor's** *sword.* **Sgt Browne** *gives* **Dermot** *the sword from the table.*

Capt Farrell   Threaten your betters?

Dermot   But I've already shown you.

Capt Farrell   In the presence of our monarch!

Cpl O'Connor   Go for his belly, Dermot, go on.

Dermot   Please, don't –

Sgt Browne   Go for his throat, lad!

Capt Skelton   Perhaps he doesn't want to fight.

Cpl O'Connor   He doesn't stand a chance, the skin-and-boned bastard, go on.

Capt Farrell   Strike me!

Dermot   What?

Cpl O'Connor   Aim for his chest!

Capt Skelton   Perhaps he'd rather settle the matter with a round of cards.

Capt Farrell   Strike me, go on!

Capt Farrell *deals a few blows at* **Dermot**, *who dodges away.*

The others laugh.

Capt Farrell   Strike me!

Dermot   But I haven't –

Capt Farrell   Go on!

Redcoats   Go on, Dermot! / His head, his head! / Hold it upright, you fool! (*Etc.*)

Capt Farrell   Are you a killer or not?

Dermot   You're not giving me a chance!

Sgt Browne   Draw your sword!

Dermot   Can we not just finish our drinks?

Skelton/Browne/O'Connor   Draw your sword!

Capt Farrell   You fucking ape, you!

He advances at **Dermot**.

Dermot *deals a pathetic blow, and instantly cowers. The* **Redcoats** *cheer.*

Capt Farrell   Is that the best you can do?

Dermot   I'm sorry, I'm sorry . . .

Capt Farrell   Is that it, you fucking infant?!

Dermot   But you're not giving me a chance.

Capt Farrell   You toddler, Dermot, what?

He again charges at **Dermot**. *They fight.*

The **Redcoats** *cheer, laugh, taunt, etc.*

Sgt Browne (*laughing, drawing his sword*)   A guinea for the first man takes his fingers!

Capt Skelton (*laughing, drawing sword*)   A guinea for his eyes!

Capt Skelton *and* **Sgt Browne** *join* **Capt Farrell** *in attacking* **Dermot**.

Dermot   God save me, help!

They all fight.

Cpl O'Connor *moves to the* **Fiddler** *and the* **Piper**, *and accompanies them, clapping his hands, stamping his foot and singing.*

During the fight, **Lieut Coyle**, *followed by* **Lieut Ryan**, *enter the tavern.*

Lieut Coyle *motions to* **Lieut Ryan** *and they sit at a table, away from the others – unseen by* **Dermot**. *The* **Pot-Boy**, *who has been roasting the piglet on the spit, moves to* **Lieuts Coyle** *and* **Ryan**, *serving them drinks.*

Cpl O'Connor (*sings*)
The corn was springing fresh and green,
And the lark sang loud and high,
And the red was on your lip, Mary,
The love light in your eye.

They say there's bread and work for all,
And the sun shines always there:
But I'll not forget old Ireland,
Were it fifty times as fair.

O'Connor/Fiddler/Piper (*sing*)
No, I'll not forget old Ireland,
Were it fifty times as . . . !

Sgt Browne *feigns being hit by* **Dermot** *and falls.*

Sgt Browne (*falls*)   Aaah!

Capt Farrell   Sergeant Browne, sir!

Sgt Browne   My leg!

Over the following, **Dermot** *tries to escape, but is caught by* **L-Cpl Finnigan,** *who drags him back to* **Capt Skelton. Capt Farrell** *attends to* **Sgt Browne**.

Capt Farrell   Are you all right?

Sgt Browne   By Christ . . .

Capt Farrell   Are you hit, Sergeant?!

Cpl O'Connor (*to the* **Fiddler**)   You play like you were scratching your hole.

Sgt Browne   He hit me in the leg, the little bastard!

Dermot   I never touched him!

Capt Skelton (*to* **Dermot**)   Stay where you are.

Cpl O'Connor (*to the* **Fiddler**)   There's a man here dying, do you wish to finish him off?

Capt Farrell   Can you walk?

Sgt Browne   May God preserve me!

Capt Farrell   Can you walk, Sergeant?

Sgt Browne (*tries to walk*)   Aaah!

Capt Farrell   He's crippled, look!

Sgt Browne   My leg, my leg!

Capt Skelton   Do you see what you've done?

Sgt Browne   Send for the gravedigger!

Cpl O'Connor   Let me help you, Sergeant, come on.

Sgt Browne   My last rites, O'Connor, I beg you.

Capt Skelton   Do you see the damage you've caused?

Dermot   Damage? But I didn't even come close –

Capt Skelton   Is this how you repay us our kindness, boy?

Capt Farrell   Bring him here.

Dermot   I hardly scratched him, look!

Capt Farrell   Bring him over, Captain.

Dermot   He's lying to you – please!

Capt Skelton and **L-Cpl Finnigan** *pull* **Dermot** *over towards* **Capt Farrell***, who is at the table.*

Cpl O'Connor *tends to* **Sgt Browne***.*

Lieuts Coyle *and* **Ryan** *continue drinking silently at their table.*

Dermot   I could hardly place my own shadow!

Capt Farrell   Look at him.

Dermot   There are five against one here, you can't expect me to –

Capt Farrell   Take a good look.

Capt Skelton   Is it your pleasure to murder members of His Majesty's armed forces?

Dermot   What?

Capt Skelton   Is it your will and intention to murder members of – ?

Dermot   I never touched him!

Capt Farrell   Did they send you?

Dermot   Who?

Capt Farrell *strikes* **Dermot***.*

Capt Farrell   Traitor!

Capt Skelton *strikes* **Dermot***.*

Capt Skelton   Catholic bastard, they sent you, didn't they?

Dermot   Who?

Capt Farrell   The whiteshirts!

Dermot   What whiteshirts?

Capt Skelton   Sent to violate Brown Bess.

Dermot   But I don't know any –

Capt Farrell   We should burn him at the stake.

Sgt Browne   Take his poisonous tongue out!

Capt Farrell   Damned insurgent, you!

Sgt Browne   Bring me his tongue and he can lick my wound!

Capt Skelton   Who sent you?

Dermot   Boys, please . . .

Sgt Browne (*to the* **Pot-Boy**)   Bring me a drink, you ape!

Capt Skelton   Who sent you?

Sgt Browne (*to the* **Pot-Boy**)   Leave that damn pig alone!

Over the following, the **Pot-Boy**, *who has returned to the spit and begun removing the piglet, quickly dumps it on the table and pours a drink for* **Sgt Browne**.

Capt Skelton   Who sent you?

Capt Farrell   Was it the Whiteshirts?

Capt Skelton   Give me their names!

Dermot   What whiteshirts?

Capt Skelton   Their names!

Dermot   But I don't know who you mean!

Capt Skelton   Tell us about your man!

Dermot   I don't know any whiteshirts!

Capt Skelton   Tell us about your benefactor!

Capt Farrell   Was he a man or a fish?

Capt Skelton   I'll wager he was neither.

Sgt Browne   A guinea for your bet!

Capt Skelton   Are you mocking us?

Dermot   But I told you already –

Capt Farrell   Was he human?

Dermot   Human?

Capt Skelton   Did he go by a name?

Capt Farrell   Was he a man?

Dermot   Yes!

Capt Farrell   Was he a man?

Dermot   Yes!

Capt Farrell   Was he a tall man?

Dermot   Who?

Capt Farrell *strikes* **Dermot**.

Dermot   I don't know, sir!

Capt Farrell   What?

Dermot   Yes!

Capt Farrell   What was he?

Dermot   He was the tallest man I ever did see!

They laugh.

But he was!

Capt Skelton   Are you certain?

Dermot   I swear to you!

Sgt Browne   God help you, child!

Dermot   He was ten foot tall and climbing if he was any man at all!

They laugh.

Capt Skelton (*affects English accent*)   Oh, I expect he was a very giant, Your Honour.

Sgt Browne (*laughing*)   He'd crush you with his bare arse, he would!

Dermot   He would!

Cpl O'Connor   Oh, I doubt he was mortal at all.

Capt Farrell   Was he not one of Satan's creatures, I wonder?

Capt Skelton   Did you get a good look at his face?

Dermot   His face?

Capt Farrell   What colour was he, boy?

Dermot   Which colour would you like?

Capt Farrell *slaps* **Dermot**.

Capt Farrell   What colour was he?

Cpl O'Connor   He doesn't sound like anyone I know.

Capt Farrell   Was he a foreigner?

Dermot   If you want.

Capt Skelton   Answer the man.

Dermot   But did I not just – ?

Capt Skelton *slaps* **Dermot**.

Cpl O'Connor   Did he crawl from out your hole?

Dermot   But I don't understand . . .

Sgt Browne   A soldier, he claims!

Dermot   I'm here, aren't I?

Sgt Browne   Fine soldiery to strike at his own kind!

Dermot   I'm here, look!

Capt Skelton   Oh, you're here all right.

Dermot   Just tell me what you want and I will give it to you!

Capt Skelton   You're one of us now, Dermot.

Dermot   I give you my pig!

Sgt Browne   Jesus Christ, lad . . .

Dermot   I give you my pig. I give you my pig!

Dermot *breaks free from* **Capts Skelton** *and* **Farrell**, *grabbing the roasted piglet from off the table – it is very hot.*

They laugh.

Dermot   I give it to you, sir, please!

The **Pot-Boy** *tries to retrieve the piglet.*

Dermot   Let go of me!

Dermot *and the* **Pot-Boy** *wrestle over the piglet, the* **Redcoats** *laughing.*

Dermot   Get your hands off me!

Dermot *boots and beats the* **Pot-Boy** *to the ground – the* **Redcoats** *cheer.*

Dermot   I killed it for you, look!

L-Cpl Finnigan *seizes* **Dermot**, *who clutches onto the piglet.*

Dermot   By my own free will!

Capt Farrell   Free will!

Dermot   It's true, I beg you!

Capt Farrell   You were captured by my own guard – free will!

Dermot   It was I who found you!

Capt Farrell   Did you not apprehend him, Finnigan?

L-Cpl Finnigan (*clutching* **Dermot**)   That's right, sir, yes.

Dermot (*struggles*)   He's lying!

L-Cpl Finnigan   He was hiding in the pigpen as you see him now. Him and his wee dagger hidden in the swill.

Dermot (*struggles*)   No, that's not it at all!

L-Cpl Finnigan   A coward if I ever saw one.

Dermot   But I meant for you to come, it was my very will and intention to do so!

Sgt Browne   A likely story.

Dermot   Just give me your orders and I will obey!

Sgt Browne   Said the fox to the hen.

Dermot   Let me prove it to you, please!

Dermot *breaks free from* **L-Cpl Finnigan** *and falls on his knees before* **Sgt Browne**.

Dermot   Let me serve my lord and master, let me serve your honest King! It's the girl you're after having, it's my pretty little sister, not me! She conspired with my mammy to unshackle me so free! I swear they'd rob the Virgin's womb if a profit it would bring!

Capt Skelton (*to* **Browne**)   He'd claim you for his wife, Browne.

Capt Farrell   Oh, they'd make a bountiful brood, by God.

Dermot (*to* **Browne**)   Don't let them leave me here.

Cpl O'Connor   Send them to the chapel!

Sgt Browne   For God's sake, will you not yield?

Dermot (*to* **Browne**)   I was a man once, please, look at me.

Sgt Browne   Get up.

Dermot (*to* **Browne**)   I was a man just like you.

Sgt Browne   Get up.

Dermot (*to* **Browne**)   You believe me though, don't you?

Sgt Browne   Get up, you mole.

Dermot   But, sir –

Sgt Browne   Embarrass me in front of my brothers.

Dermot   I'll kiss your feet.

Sgt Browne   What?

Dermot   I kiss your feet, sir!

Dermot *kisses* **Sgt Browne**'*s feet.*

Sgt Browne   Jesus Christ!

The others laugh.

Have you no shame, boy?!

He boots **Dermot** *away.*

Sgt Browne (*to* **Finnigan**)   Take him away, would you?

Dermot (*to* **Browne**)   You believe me though, don't you?

Sgt Browne   Send him back to Rome!

Dermot   But, sir, you have to –

Sgt Browne   Papist scum!

Dermot   You have to believe me.

Sgt Browne   I don't have to do anything, boy. (*To* **Finnigan**.)
Take him away I said!

Dermot (*sees* **Coyle**)   You believe me, don't you, Daddy?

Capt Farrell (*laughs*)   What?

Dermot   Daddy, please, you have to tell them.

Dermot *kneels at* **Lieut Coyle**'s *feet.*

Capt Farrell (*laughs*)   Am I hearing things, Skelton?

Dermot (*to* **Coyle**)   Tell them I'm no –

Lieut Coyle *pushes* **Dermot** *away.*

Lieut Coyle   Move.

Dermot   Tell them I'm no traitor.

Lieut Coyle (*pushes* **Dermot**)   Go home.

Dermot   Tell them how I only wish to serve the greater good.

Lieut Coyle   For Christ's sake . . . !

Dermot   Father, please . . .

Lieut Coyle   Go home, I said!

He hurls **Dermot** *away.*

Long pause.

Dermot   Daddy . . .

Lieut Coyle   Let a man finish his drink, would you?

Dermot   You have to tell them, please!

Lieut Coyle (*to* **Ryan**)   Pass me that jug there, would you, Ryan?

Dermot   But I killed a pig for you.

Lieut Coyle (*grabs the ale jug himself*)   For God's sake, man!

Dermot   I went to the farm, look.

Dermot *offers the roasted piglet to* **Lieut Coyle**.

Dermot   I killed a pig for you, Daddy.

Lieut Coyle   Get that thing away from me! Jesus Christ . . .

Dermot   You remember the old farm.

Lieut Coyle   I don't know what you're talking about!

Dermot   The farm they stole from us, Daddy — please.

Sgt Browne (*grabs* **Dermot**)   All right now, that's enough.

Dermot   You remember the prayers we made.

Sgt Browne (*pulls* **Dermot** *away from* **Coyle**)   Leave the man alone!

Dermot   'For in thee, O Lord, do I put my trust!'

Sgt Browne   Enough, I say!

Sgt Browne *and* **Dermot** *struggle, as* **Dermot** *tries to fight his way back to* **Lieut Coyle**'s *table.*

Dermot (*struggles*)   'Let me never be put to confusion! Deliver me in thy righteousness and cause me to – '

Capt Skelton (*strikes* **Dermot**)   Let him finish his drink, you bairn.

Dermot   'And cause me to escape!'

Capt Farrell (*strikes* **Dermot**)   You'll have to excuse the boy, Lieutenant.

Dermot   That is what you taught me! . . .

Capt Farrell   He's out of his wits from the ale.

Dermot   Tell me you haven't forgotten, tell me that! Tell them what I'm made of at least! – What, have you lost your senses?

Sgt Browne (*strikes* **Dermot**)   Watch your manners, Whiteshirt!

Dermot (*to* **Browne**)   But I've proved I can kill, I've shown you proof already!

Capt Skelton   You've certainly done that, lad.

Capt Farrell   He'd have us all spitting soil if he could.

Capt Skelton   What do you say, Coyle?

Dermot   Daddy, please . . .

Capt Farrell   Leave the man alone!

Dermot   Don't let them do this to me!

Capt Farrell *pulls* **Dermot** *away from* **Lieut Coyle**.

Capt Skelton   Well, what do you say? Come on now . . .

Dermot   After all you bid me promise.

Capt Farrell   Be quiet!

Capt Skelton   Do you not promise him a place in the regiment?

Dermot   After all the years at your service —

Capt Farrell   Be quiet, I say!

He strikes **Dermot**.

Capt Skelton   Do you not promise him a place in the regiment?

Lieut Coyle   No.

Sgt Browne   Is he not your kin?

Lieut Coyle   I've never seen him before.

Capt Skelton   Is he not your kin, Lieutenant?

Pause.

Lieutenant . . .

Lieut Coyle   No.

Sgt Browne   Does he lie to us?

Lieut Coyle   He's nothing.

Capt Skelton   Are you certain?

Lieut Coyle   He's nothing, I say! – Dear God, Skelton!

Capt Skelton   What did I tell you?

Dermot   But I swear to you, no!

Lieut Coyle   Do I have to grovel at your fucking feet?

Capt Skelton   Treachery.

Dermot   I swear to you, on my life I do!.

Capt Farrell   Stop your noise.

Dermot   You don't mean that!

Capt Farrell   That's enough!

Dermot   He doesn't mean that.

Cpl O'Connor   Oh come now, Dermot –

Dermot   He doesn't mean that, look!

Cpl O'Connor   The Lieutenant makes no claims on you.

Dermot   Look into his eyes!

Cpl O'Connor   Now if you want us to be merciful . . .

Sgt Browne   Merciful my two balls!

Dermot   But I know he doesn't.

Sgt Browne   Finish the bastard!

Dermot   He doesn't mean what he says, he wouldn't do that to me.

Sgt Browne   Take his head off, Captain!

Dermot   His only living son, he wouldn't –

Cpl O'Connor   His head, his head!

Dermot   He wouldn't let that happen! Daddy, no!

Lieut Coyle   All right now, just –

Sgt Browne   Take it off, for the love of God, take it off!

Dermot *faints.*

Sgt Browne   I'm sick of hearing him squeal!

He grabs **Dermot** *and draws his sword.*

Sgt Browne   Dirty heathen bastard, you.

Lieut Coyle   That's enough now, Sergeant!

Sgt Browne   Try to infiltrate our honest —

Lieut Coyle   That's enough, I beg you – stop!

Lieut Coyle *comes between* **Sgt Browne** *and* **Dermot***, drawing his sword.*

Pause.

Lieut Coyle   Jesus Christ, Browne . . .

Sgt Browne   Put down your weapon, sir.

Lieut Coyle   Have you not punished the boy enough?

Sgt Browne   Put it down.

Lieut Coyle   Can't you see he meant no harm?

Sgt Browne   Threaten me with your blunt metal!

He strikes **Lieut Coyle***'s sword away.*

Capt Farrell   All right now, boys . . .

Sgt Browne   What are you?!

Pause.

Lieut Coyle   Look . . .

Sgt Browne   What are you, Coyle?!

Sgt Browne *strikes* **Lieut Coyle***'s sword.*

Lieut Coyle   Just let me talk to him.

Sgt Browne   Are you his fucking pimp that you stand in the way of your own brothers?!

Sgt Browne *strikes at* **Lieut Coyle** *a couple of times.* **Lieut Coyle** *blocking him.*

Capt Farrell   Steady on now, Browne.

Sgt Browne   Are you his pimp, sir?!

Lieut Coyle   Forgive me, just –

Capt Skelton   Perhaps you'd care for us to step aside, sir, no?

Lieut Coyle   He's not worth such trouble – Captain, please.

Capt Farrell   Would you like some privacy?

Lieut Coyle   I'm certain he didn't mean to harm anyone . . .

Sgt Browne   He's a traitor, Lieutenant!

Lieut Coyle   He needs a doctor, that's all.

Sgt Browne   He needs what?

Lieut Coyle   Just let me speak with him a minute, Sergeant.

Sgt Browne   The end of my sword!

Lieut Coyle   But I can prove it . . .

Sgt Browne   The gaol, Lieutenant!

Lieut Coyle   Let me prove it to you, damn it!

He strikes **Sgt Browne**'s *sword away with his own.*

Cpl O'Connor   Oh come now, Coyle, we were only having a little fun with the boy.

Lieut Coyle   Dermot, please . . .

Capt Farrell (*to the* **Pot-Boy**)   A round of drinks here, lad!

Lieut Coyle   Come on now, child, get up off the floor.

He crouches down by the unconscious **Dermot**.

Sgt Browne   Jesus save us!

Lieut Coyle   Get up, Dermot, come on.

Sgt Browne (*to* **Skelton**)   Are you just going to stand there?

Lieut Coyle   For God's sake, wake up!

Cpl O'Connor   I think we found our answer, Browne.

Lieut Coyle   Wake up, I say!

Capt Skelton   He needs a doctor all right.

Lieut Coyle   Dermot, please . . .

Sgt Browne   I can stand this no more.

Lieut Coyle   Don't make a fool of me now!

Sgt Browne *pulls* **Lieut Coyle** *away from* **Dermot**.

Sgt Browne   Pull yourself together, Coyle!

Lieut Coyle   Don't do this, child!

Sgt Browne   On your feet now, be a man!

Lieut Coyle   For Christ's sake, Browne –

Capt Farrell   Let him go.

Lieut Coyle   – can you not think without your fists for one minute?!

Capt Farrell   Behave yourselves, the pair of you!

Lieut Coyle   Captain Farrell, please . . .

Capt Farrell   At ease, Lieutenant.

Lieut Coyle   But I only –

Capt Farrell   At ease!

Lieut Coyle   But if you would just give me one moment –

Capt Farrell   Do you want to shame the whole regiment?

Lieut Coyle   But I only want you to think twice before –

Sgt Browne   The boy's a traitor!

Lieut Coyle   You don't know that, Sergeant.

Sgt Browne   It came from his own two lips!

Lieut Coyle   Captain Farrell, come on now!

Sgt Browne   I know what I heard!

Lieut Coyle   You know that if we might just speak reasonably . . .

Sgt Browne   Reasonably he says!

Cpl O'Connor   Wake up, you toad, you heard the man!

He kicks the unconscious **Dermot**.

Lieut Coyle   Jesus Christ, don't –

Cpl O'Connor   Explain yourself!

He kicks **Dermot**.

Lieut Coyle   O'Connor, don't –

Sgt Browne   On your feet, traitor!

He boots **Dermot**.

Lieut Coyle   Would you please stop . . . ?!

Sgt Browne *and* **Cpl O'Connor** *boot* **Dermot**.

Lieut Coyle   Stop this madness! Tell them to stop, Captain!

Capt Skelton   Can you vouch for him?

Lieut Coyle   Let him stand trial at least!

Capt Skelton   Then you would speak for him, Lieutenant.

Capt Farrell   You think he's innocent.

Lieut Coyle   I hardly know the boy!

Capt Skelton   And your defence?

Long pause.

And your defence?

Lieut Coyle   Look . . .

Capt Farrell   Speak up, Coyle.

Lieut Coyle   He's no threat to any one of us, Captain.

Cpl O'Connor   So you do know him?

Lieut Coyle   He's an animal, he should never have set foot in this place.

Sgt Browne   Did you lie to us?

Lieut Coyle   Of course not!

Sgt Browne   Did he not lie, Corporal?

Lieut Coyle   I only meant . . .

Capt Farrell   You don't sound too sure.

Lieut Coyle   I know him from the town, sir, that's all! Surely you must have seen him yourselves?

Capt Skelton   Have you seen him, Farrell?

Lieut Coyle   I've seen him hiding out in the forest, Captain, he's a scavenger, that's all. He's lived here all his life, he doesn't know right from wrong, it's his breeding.

Capt Farrell   He seems to know you, sir.

Lieut Coyle   He has me mistaken.

Capt Farrell   Did you not apprehend him then?

Lieut Coyle   What?

Capt Skelton   In the forest.

Lieut Coyle   I think it was the forest.

Capt Skelton   You let him go?

Lieut Coyle   I don't remember –

Capt Skelton   You just said so, Coyle! In the forest!

Capt Farrell   When in the forest?

Lieut Coyle   Don't make me repeat myself, Captain Farrell. I just told you, he's an idiot.

Capt Farrell   Answer the question!

Lieut Coyle   A harmless idiot – what good would a trial do? Yes, I pitied him! I pitied him as I would a stray dog, wouldn't you also? So I gave him a little meat from my plate, so what?! The boy obviously has no family to speak of – For all I know he might come from any of your noble blood.

Capt Skelton   But it's you he calls Father.

Lieut Coyle   He'd give a rat the same title, come on with you!

Capt Farrell   And the witch?

Sgt Browne   The witch is his mistress, I warrant.

Lieut Coyle   The witch is his own brain!

Capt Skelton (*laughs*)   It's his what now?

Lieut Coyle   His brain, Captain Skelton, you know what I mean! It's the product of his breeding.

Capt Farrell   But you swore he had no such thing.

Lieut Coyle   I swore nothing of the sort! For God's sake, Ryan, will you not speak?!

He marches over to **Lieut Ryan***, who remains seated.*

Lieut Coyle   Speak up, damn you!

Lieut Ryan   But, sir –

Lieut Coyle *strikes* **Lieut Ryan***.*

Lieut Coyle   Dumb bastard, what have I taught you?

Capt Skelton   Now, Coyle . . .

Lieut Coyle   Tell them I'm no hypocrite – speak up!

Capt Skelton   That's enough now, don't –

Lieut Coyle   What have I taught you, boy?!

Lieut Ryan   I can't say, sir, I –

Lieut Coyle   What have I taught you?! – Come on!

Cpl O'Connor   Do you have something to tell us, Ryan?

Lieut Coyle   Come on now, will you not defend your master?

Cpl O'Connor   Well?

Lieut Coyle   Don't just sit there – haven't we served together long enough?

Capt Skelton   Let him speak for himself, Coyle.

Cpl O'Connor   Would you defend him?

Lieut Coyle (*to* **Ryan**)   If it's your uncle you're worried about –

Capt Farrell   Lieutenant Ryan!

Lieut Ryan   No, sir.

Capt Farrell   Does he tell us the truth?

Lieut Ryan   He does not, sir, no! He's a liar and a traitor!

Sgt Browne (*laughs*)   Oh!

Lieut Ryan   I've seen him with my own two eyes!

Lieut Coyle   God help you, boy.

Lieut Ryan   Him and the witch, sir, on my honour!

Sgt Browne (*laughs*)   Honour, indeed!

Lieut Ryan   They do lie like lovers in the forest!

Lieut Coyle   God help you to your death.

Cpl O'Connor (*to* **Ryan**)   Oh, that takes some balls, lad, go on with you!

Lieut Coyle   God help you, you ungrateful little bastard!

Lieut Coyle *goes for* **Lieut Ryan**.

Lieut Ryan   Don't you touch me!

Lieut Coyle   I swear on your unborn children!

Capt Farrell   You swear nothing, Coyle!

He seizes **Lieut Coyle**.

Lieut Coyle   They'll finish you, spoiled brat! You decoration you!

Capt Farrell   That's an order!

Lieut Coyle   You won't last a second in that war!

Capt Farrell *strikes* **Lieut Coyle**.

Lieut Coyle   Aah!

Capt Farrell   That's an order, Coyle — let him go!

Sgt Browne (*to the* **Pot-Boy**)   You there!

Capt Farrell (*to* **Coyle**)   If you so much as mark this boy . . .

Lieut Coyle   He is my responsibility!

Cpl O'Connor (*to the* **Pot-Boy**)   Fill up his booze, lad, go on!

Sgt Browne (*to the* **Pot-Boy**)   Go on with you, hurry!

Capt Skelton (*to* **Finnigan**, *of* **Dermot**)   Mop up this beast, would you, Finnigan?

Cpl O'Connor (*hands* **Ryan** *a pipe*)   Have my pipe – that's it, put your feet up!

Capt Farrell (*to* **Coyle**)   Don't struggle with me now, Coyle, you've been named.

Lieut Coyle   Jesus Christ, Farrell, can't you see he's – ?

Capt Farrell *strikes* **Lieut Coyle**.

Capt Farrell   Shut your mouth!

Lieut Coyle   Can't you see he's frightened out his wits? He'll say anything –

Capt Farrell   He'll speak before the Colonel – stay down!

Lieut Coyle   How long have we known each other, eh?

Sgt Browne   Not long enough, it seems!

Lieut Coyle   But, Sergeant Browne, you know that I would never –

Sgt Browne   Lying dog!

He winds **Lieut Coyle**.

Lieut Coyle   Ooh!

Sgt Browne   You and your dirty pigling!

Capt Skelton (*to* **Finnigan**)   Take him to the gaol, man, go on!

Capt Farrell (*to* **Finnigan**)   Take his eyes out, you hear?!

L-Cpl Finnigan *takes* **Dermot**, *who is beginning to wake, by his legs and proceeds to drag him to the exit.*

Lieut Coyle   But, Captain, please, you really don't have to do this . . .

Dermot (*waking, to* **Finnigan**)   Let go of me, oh!

Capt Skelton   Let him wake the beggar blind!

Cpl O'Connor   Can we not have some music here, you scum?

Cpl O'Connor *strikes the* **Fiddler** *and* **Piper** *who begin to play.*

Dermot (*struggles*)   Let go of me, I said!

Lieut Coyle   He's just a boy, please . . .

Dermot (*struggles*)   Let go! Oh, help, help!

Dermot *struggles as* **L-Cpl Finnigan** *tries to drag him out.*

Dermot   Daddy, save me!

Lieut Coyle   He's just a boy for Christ's sake! For Christ's sake, will you not . . . ?!

Lieut Coyle *breaks free from* **Capt Farrell** *and attacks the* **Redcoats** *with his sword.*

Capt Farrell   Seize him!

Lieut Coyle *and the* **Redcoats** *fight.*

Capt Farrell   Seize him, Corporal!

Lieut Coyle   Run away, Dermot, run!

Dermot *grabs the piglet and exits, charging out of the cabin. He is pursued by* **L-Cpl Finnigan**, *who also exits.*

The others fight.

During the fight, the **Pot-Boy** *is accidently hit by a sword.*

Over the rest of the scene, the **Pot-Boy** *is left to die, blood pouring from his wound.*

Capt Skelton   Take him down, Sergeant!

Capt Farrell   Hit him in the gut!

Capt Skelton   Take him down!

Capt Farrell   The gut, his guts!

Sgt Browne   Treacherous old fool!

The **Redcoats** *knock* **Lieut Coyle**'s *sword out of his hands and push him to the ground.*

Lieut Coyle   Aaaah!

Capt Farrell   Hold him down!

Lieut Coyle *tries to break free.*

Capt Farrell   Hold him down, Corporal, move!

Over the following, **Cpl O'Connor**, **Capt Skelton** *and* **Sgt Browne** *pin* **Lieut Coyle** *to one of the chairs.*

Lieut Coyle   For Christ's sake, show some mercy!

Sgt Browne   And whose mercy is that, Coyle?

Lieut Coyle   Are we not of the same stuff?

Sgt Browne   The mercy of your Pope?

Lieut Coyle   We are made of the same blood, Captain!

Capt Skelton   But I thought you'd never met the boy!

Sgt Browne   They're star-crossed lovers, by Jove!

Lieut Coyle   You know what I mean, damn you!

Cpl O'Connor (*laughs, to the musicians*)   A ballad for his holiness! A ballad, a ballad! Soften your bow!

Pot-Boy   May the Devil fuck you all!

Lieut Coyle   We are all of us made of the same flesh and blood, you know that!

Capt Farrell   Oh, we are?

Lieut Coyle   You know that, sir!

Capt Skelton   Hold him down, Corporal.

Lieut Coyle   All of you fucking hypocrites . . .

Pot-Boy   May he fuck your mothers all!

The **Redcoats** *struggle to keep* **Lieut Coyle** *down on his seat.*

Sgt Browne   Stay down!

Lieut Coyle   You were all of you born Catholic – do you think I don't know that? Every last one of you! You only converted out of fear, for all I know you still practise it to this day!

Capt Farrell   Hold your tongue!

He strikes **Lieut Coyle** *across the face with his cup.*

Lieut Coyle   Aah!

Capt Farrell   Hold your tongue unless it's a confession you do speak.

Capt Skelton   Take his legs, Sergeant.

Sgt Browne (*moves to* **Coyle**)   Dirty vermin, you.

Capt Skelton   Draw the blood to his head, go on.

Sgt Browne   Make a mockery of our trust!

Over the next, **Cpl O'Connor** *and* **Sgt Browne** *pull a struggling* **Lieut Coyle** *by his feet, and hang him upside down.*

Lieut Coyle   No, please!

Capt Farrell   Don't struggle now, boy!

Lieut Coyle   Please, don't do this!

Capt Skelton   Lift him up, I said!

Lieut Coyle   But I swear to you, boys, I swear!

Cpl O'Connor   Does he swear, do you think?

Lieut Coyle   You're making a terrible mistake, on my life! As God is my witness, I swear to you, I would never betray you!

Lieut Coyle, *upside down, is kicked in the head by* **Capt Skelton**.

Capt Skelton   Swear to the King of England!

Lieut Coyle   The King of England!

Capt Skelton   Swear it!

He kicks **Lieut Coyle** *in the head.*

Capt Farrell   Are you lying to us again? He's lying to us again!

Capt Skelton   Lieutenant Coyle!

Lieut Coyle   I swear!

Capt Farrell   He's all gas, look!

Capt Skelton   Are you prepared to die for your King?

Pause.

Lieutenant Thomas Coyle . . .

Capt Farrell   Answer the man!

Capt Skelton   Are you prepared to die for your King?

Lieut Coyle   You know I am!

Capt Skelton   Call yourself a soldier.

Lieut Coyle   Jesus Christ . . .

Capt Skelton *strikes* **Lieut Coyle** *across the face.*

Lieut Coyle   Aah!

Capt Skelton   Speak!

Capt Farrell   Catholic worm, you.

Cpl O'Connor   Answer the question.

Capt Skelton *strikes* **Lieut Coyle** *twice about the face.*

Lieut Coyle   I am!

Capt Skelton   Are you prepared to die –

Lieut Coyle   I am!

Capt Skelton   – for your King?

Lieut Coyle   I am, I am!

Cpl O'Connor *and* **Sgt Browne** *throw* **Lieut Coyle** *to the ground – crash.*

Lieut Coyle   Aaaahh!

The **Redcoats** *laugh.*

Lieut Coyle   Are you trying to fucking cripple me too?

Sgt Browne   Is that shit coming off him?

Cpl O'Connor   He's soiled himself, look!

Sgt Browne   God save us, Captain Farrell!

Capt Farrell   We should get him out of these clothes then, boys!

Capt Farrell *grabs* **Lieut Coyle**.

Lieut Coyle   No! No, wait, please!!

Lieut Coyle, *struggling, has his uniform ripped off him by the* **Redcoats**, *leaving him in just his undergarments.*

Lieut Coyle   Please, stop!

Capt Skelton   On your feet!

Lieut Coyle   Stop this madness! I promise you I'll –

Sgt Browne   On your fucking feet!

Lieut Coyle   I'll die for you, I promise!

The **Redcoats** *pull* **Lieut Coyle**, *in just his undergarments, to his feet. On his throat hangs a silver chain, off which hangs the crucifix.*

Sgt Browne   I think we found our answer, boys!

Lieut Coyle   I promise you, dear God! Dear God, I would never —

Sgt Browne *rips off the chain/crucifix.*

Lieut Coyle   Agh!

Sgt Browne   The King of the Jews no less!

Capt Farrell   And the meek shall inherit the Earth!

He rummages through **Lieut Coyle***'s uniform.*

Cpl O'Connor   God help you, Coyle. You must know you're forbidden to wear such tokens.

Lieut Coyle   It isn't mine.

Capt Skelton   You violate the law.

Lieut Coyle   It was given to me – I beg you.

Capt Skelton   What?

Lieut Coyle   I forgot I even had the damn thing.

Capt Skelton   And did one of your allies give you this?

Cpl O'Connor   Surely you know better than to wear it on your person?

Capt Farrell *discovers the missal.*

Lieut Coyle   But I wasn't –

Capt Farrell   The man's armed, I warrant!

Sgt Browne   The man's a fool!

Capt Farrell   For my sins, that he would carry a prayer book too!

Lieut Coyle   But I was only holding them for someone.

Capt Skelton   Someone who?

Lieut Coyle   They don't belong to me, they're not –

Capt Skelton   Someone who, Lieutenant? A priest?

Cpl O'Connor   A Jesuit, I warrant.

Capt Farrell   Would you like to hear a passage, Coyle?

Lieut Coyle   But I was about to get rid of them –

Sgt Browne   Here's your passage right enough!

Sgt Browne *reaches under* **Lieut Coyle**'s *long johns, shoving the chain/crucifix up* **Lieut Coyle**'s *arse.*

Lieut Coyle   Aaah!

The **Redcoats** *laugh.*

Capt Farrell (*laughs*)   Oh, forgive me, Father, please!

Sgt Browne   Hand me that prayer book, Farrell!

Capt Farrell (*laughs*)   They know not what they do!

Sgt Browne   Let me anoint it, come on!

Sgt Browne *snatches the prayer book from* **Capt Farrell**. *Over the following, he takes it to the corner of the tavern and pisses on it.*

Lieut Coyle (*to* **Skelton**)   I beg you, please, I didn't –

Capt Skelton *flogs* **Lieut Coyle** *with his sword.*

Capt Skelton   You didn't what?

Lieut Coyle   I didn't think, I didn't think –

Capt Skelton *flogs* **Lieut Coyle** *with his sword.*

Capt Skelton   You didn't think, Coyle, come on!

Lieut Coyle   But I would never in my dreams –

Capt Skelton   You didn't think, Coyle, you didn't think!

He flogs **Lieut Coyle** *several times, bringing him to his knees.*

Lieut Ryan *watches from his chair, uncomfortably smoking his pipe.*

The **Pot-Boy** *continues to bleed to death.*

Capt Skelton   Out with it, man! What, have you lost your tongue?!

Lieut Coyle   I told you, I'm not –

Capt Farrell *and* **Cpl O'Connor** *flog* **Lieut Coyle**.

Lieut Coyle   Jesus save me!

Capt Skelton   Let's hear you, traitor!

Lieut Coyle   Brothers, please, my allegiance is with the King!

Capt Farrell   Would you sing for our King?

Lieut Coyle   I swear to you –

Capt Farrell   Would you sing?

Capt Skelton   Would you sing the Hymn of Old England, would you sing?

Cpl O'Connor   Lieutenant Coyle!

Lieut Coyle   But you know that I wouldn't –

Sgt Browne (*returns with the soaked missal*)   Sing, you damn imposter!

Lieut Coyle   In all our time together, have I ever – ?

Sgt Browne *rips a page from out of the missal and shoves it in* **Lieut Coyle**'s *mouth.*

Sgt Browne   Let's hear you, come on!

Lieut Coyle   Boys, please!

The **Redcoats** *pull* **Lieut Coyle** *to his feet.*

Lieut Coyle   Please, you can't –

Capt Farrell   On your feet!

Lieut Coyle   Don't do this to me. I'm not the one you're after, it's –

Sgt Browne *stuffs the missal into* **Lieut Coyle**'s *mouth and throat.*

Sgt Browne   Sing the Hymn of Britannia!

Cpl O'Connor   Sing along, come on!

Redcoats (*sing*)
    God bless our Lord the King!
    God save our Lord the King!
    God save our King!

As they sing, **Lieut Coyle** *struggles to break free, while the* **Redcoats** *flog and jab him with their swords.*

Redcoats (*sing*)
Make him victorious,
Happy and glorious,
Long to reign over us,
God bless our King!

Lieut Coyle *collapses. They laugh.*

Over the next, **Capt Skelton** *takes* **Lieut Coyle***'s jacket, and drapes it over* **Lieut Ryan***'s shoulders.*

Capt Farrell (*kicks* **Coyle**)   On your feet!

Sgt Browne (*kicks* **Coyle**)   Get up!

Cpl O'Connor (*kicks* **Coyle**)   Get up, Lieutenant!

Sgt Browne (*kicks* **Coyle**)   Prove yourself, come on with you!

Sgt Browne *boots* **Lieut Coyle** *in the face.*

Capt Skelton (*to* **Ryan**)   Your dog seems to have lost his tongue, Lieutenant.

Blackout.

Four

The cabin.

Night.

The storm continues.

Ellen *crouches on the floor.* **Maryanne***, her face slashed and semi-conscious, has her head resting on her daughter's lap.* **Ellen** *is trying to feed her soup from a bowl.*

Ellen   Mammy.

Pause.

Mammy, please.

Long pause.

Mammy, please, drink up.

Pause.

Drink up.

Pause.

Drink it, Mammy, please, I made it for you.

Thunder and lightning.

Pause.

I cooked it up special, look.

Pause.

I used the blood from out the pig – please, you'll need all the strength you can get.

Thunder and lightning.

Come on, Mammy, the colour's draining from your cheeks.

Pause.

Come on, Mammy, you're not even trying!

*She punches **Maryanne**'s chest.*

Ellen   You've got to work harder, please!

*She punches **Maryanne**'s chest.*

Pause.

*She checks **Maryanne**'s heartbeat.*

Long pause.

Ellen   That's it.

Pause.

That's it now, open wide.

She feeds **Maryanne** *the soup.*

Ellen   Swallow.

Pause.

There's a good mammy, that's right. We'll soon be back on our feet now, won't we?

Pause.

Back on our feet and ready for Daddy's return.

Pause.

Back on our feet for the feast. Ready for Easter, Mammy, that's right, just . . . What?

She leans into **Maryanne***.*

Ellen   What's that?

Pause.

You'll have to speak up, Mammy, I can barely make you out.

Pause.

Has he what?

Pause.

Oh no, I don't think so.

Pause.

No, I don't think he'll be coming back just yet. Not until he's finished packing I shouldn't think.

Pause.

That's right, Mammy, yes. He'll be packing our ball gowns as we speak, imagine that!

Pause.

Imagine that now, won't you? Our beautiful pink ball gowns, Mammy! In our jewels and sweet perfumes! The both of us, look! In our chariot the shape of a swan!

Thunder and lightning.

Enter **Dermot***, clutching onto the roasted piglet. He stands in the doorway of the cabin, unseen by* **Ellen***. The chains remain attached to his ankles, but unfastened, allowing him to move freely.*

Long pause.

Ellen   Mammy?

Long pause.

Mammy, wake up.

Dermot   We should go now.

Ellen   Would you like me to pray for you?

Dermot   We should go now, Ellen.

Ellen   You'd like that, wouldn't you?

Pause.

Dermot   Ellen . . .

Ellen (*recites*)   'And I saw a new heaven and a new earth: for the first heaven and the first earth were passed away; and there was no more sea. And I saw the holy city, new Jerusalem, coming down from God out of heaven, as a bride adorned for her husband. And I heard a great voice out of heaven saying, Behold, the tabernacle of God is with men, and he will dwell with them, and they shall be his people, and God himself shall be with them and be their God.'

Pause.

Ellen/Dermot   'And God shall wipe all the tears away from their eyes; and there shall be no more death, neither sorrow nor crying, neither shall there be any more pain: for the former things are passed away. And he that sat upon the throne said, Behold, I make all things new.'

Thunder and lightning.

Pause.

Ellen (*to* **Maryanne**)   Finish it off now, Mammy, come on.

Long pause.

Dermot   Ellen . . .

Ellen (*to* **Maryanne**)   You want to keep your health for the voyage.

Long pause.

Back on your feet for the Palace, that's it.

Dermot   Ellen . . .

Ellen   Buckingham Palace. You remember how we dreamed of the life to come?

Dermot   Ellen, look at me.

Ellen   Quiet!

Dermot   I think –

Ellen   Quiet, I say!

Dermot   I think we should go now, please.

Ellen *continues feeding* **Maryanne**.

Pause.

Dermot   We should go now, Ellen.

Ellen   Would you let me finish?!

Dermot   But –

Ellen   Let me finish, Dermot – no!

Dermot   They're coming for us.

Ellen   You're not supposed to be here!

Dermot   They're coming for me, listen! They're burning down the cabins, Ellen, will you not see?!

Ellen   Mammy said –

Dermot   Take a look if you don't believe me!

Ellen   Mammy said you're not to be here any more, she said so.

Dermot   But, sister, you're not –

Ellen   You're supposed to be a soldier now, Dermot – go on!

Dermot   Sister, please . . .

Ellen   Don't come near me. I said, you're not welcome!

Long pause.

The stench on you.

Dermot   I'm telling you, Ellen –

Ellen   Did you do it?

Dermot   She's deceived us, I swear.

Ellen   Did you free the pigs?

Dermot   What?

Ellen   Mammy told you to go to the farm, did you free them?

Dermot   Of course!

Ellen   Did you free the chickens?

Pause.

The chickens, Dermot. Did you free them from their blood?

Pause.

Don't make me use the stick.

Dermot   Yes, miss.

Ellen   And the sheep?

Dermot   Yes, miss.

Ellen   And the cows?

Pause.

And the cows, Dermot, answer me!

Dermot   Of course I freed the cows, I freed them all! I freed one just for you here – look!

He offers the piglet to **Ellen**.

Dermot   I freed her for you, Ellen.

Pause.

Look on her, won't you?

Ellen   Fibber.

Dermot   I picked her from the litter especially.

Ellen   You're always fibbing.

Dermot (*as the piglet*)   'Hello, Ellen.'

Ellen   But Mammy said –

Dermot (*as the piglet*)   'Hello, little sweet one. Daisy's the name.' Oh, she is a pretty one though, isn't she? See how she dances – look.

He plays with the piglet.

(*As the piglet.*) 'Hello, little girl-girl, hello, hello, hello. Won't you be my best friend?'

Ellen   Dermot, please . . .

Dermot (*as the piglet*)   'Daisy's the name.'

Ellen   Stop it, I say! That's not funny!

Dermot   But we may take her with us to the bog. We may hide among the reeds together. You'd like that, wouldn't you, Daisy? 'Oh, yes please, Dermot, yes please . . .'

Ellen   Stop lying to me, Dermot!

Dermot   But –

Ellen   It's me she needs . . .

She grabs the piglet off **Dermot**, *clutching on to it.*

Ellen   Leave it alone!

She continues feeding **Maryanne** *while holding the piglet to her chest.*

Long pause.

Dermot   Is she wounded?

Ellen (*to* **Maryanne**)   Mind you don't spill now.

Dermot   He did this to her, didn't he?

Ellen   Mind the wee drippy drops, that's it.

Dermot   It was Daddy, wasn't it?

Ellen   Just a few more . . .

Dermot   Tell me the truth, Ellen! He took his metal to her, didn't he? What, won't you speak? Who did this?!

Ellen   Don't be scared now, Mammy, it's only Dermot.

Dermot   Then I suppose it was the thunder, was it?!

Ellen   There's nothing to be afraid of.

Dermot   The thunder and the lightning struck her down! Is that what you'd like me to believe? I'll believe anything, you know that. It was the thunder, I knew it!

Ellen (*to* **Maryanne**)   That's it, Mammy . . .

Dermot   Is this what you'd like me to believe?!

Ellen   . . . one mouthful at a time.

Dermot   Should we choose the thunder?!

Ellen (*to* **Maryanne**)   Don't you worry about a –

Dermot   Let us believe that, Ellen, let us leave this place! Come on now, it's as good a game as any!

Ellen   You're scaring her.

Dermot   Ellen, please . . .

Ellen   She needs me – stop!

Dermot   It's going to strike every last one of us down, I tell you, we can't stay here!

L-Cpl Finnigan (*off, in the distance*)   Ho there!

Dermot   What, are you deaf? It's getting closer – listen!

L-Cpl Finnigan (*off*)   Show yourself, little bastard you, ho! It's your stink that gives you away!

Dermot *dashes over to* **Ellen**.

Dermot   Oh, won't you come with me, sister?

Ellen   I'm supposed to wait here with my mammy.

Dermot   But we haven't any time.

Ellen   I'm to wait till daybreak.

Dermot (*goes to touch* **Ellen**)   Ellen, please . . .

Ellen   Keep your hands off me! I'm to be a good girl!

Dermot   Won't you listen?!

Ellen   Stay away from me, Dermot!

Dermot   For the good of us both! Look at what they've done to me already! I swear to you, on my heart . . .

Ellen   My heart is with Daddy.

Dermot   Daddy's dead.

Ellen *stops feeding* **Maryanne**.

Long pause.

Ellen *begins plaiting* **Maryanne**'*s hair.*

Dermot   Come and play with me, Ellen, please.

Pause.

We could hide by the bog and watch the storm together.

Pause.

You remember the bog? You remember I used to take you there when you were just a bairn? We could go there now.

Pause.

We could pray to the saints together.

Pause.

We could call upon the Pope. Remember our special prayer?

Pause.

I remember.

Pause.

I remember when we might still walk freely upon this land.

Pause.

I remember how she used to carry me in her arms. And I just a babe. As you are now, Ellen, look.

Pause.

She would carry me to the river and we'd whisper of Saint Ita.

Pause.

She'd whisper me the life to come. Of how we might never face Purgatory. Of how we might yet remain free, no matter what they

stole from us. Of how we might never lose sight of each other,
Ellen – well?

Long pause.

Let me take you in my arms.

Long pause.

Ellen.

Long pause.

Ellen, please, we may still have each other.

Ellen   But Mammy said so.

Dermot   Mammy is corrupted, look! Look at her! What are you
crying for?

Ellen   She promised she would never leave me.

Dermot   Don't you cry for her.

Ellen   But she did, she did!

Dermot   Don't you do it now, child, I'm warning you!

He tries to pull **Ellen** *away from* **Maryanne**.

Dermot   For the love of God, don't –

Ellen   Ow!

Dermot   Don't do this, I swear to you, don't –

Pounding at the cabin door.

Oh Jesus Christ, oh no!

He leaps onto **Ellen**, *covering her mouth.*

Ellen *struggles to break free.*

Dermot   Stay down, will you?!

Ellen   Dermot, please, you're hurting me!

Dermot   Be quiet, Ellen, be quiet!

Ellen   Get off me, you're not –

Pounding at the cabin door.

L-Cpl Finnigan (*off*)   You there, open this door!

Ellen *tries to break free, but* **Dermot** *suppresses her.*

L-Cpl Finnigan (*off*)   Open this door I say – ho!

Pounding at the cabin door.

Dermot *drags a struggling* **Ellen** *to the cabin door and presses their weight against it.*

L-Cpl Finnigan (*off*)   In the name of our King!

L-Cpl Finnigan, *offstage, tries booting the cabin door open.* **Dermot**, *with* **Ellen**, *keeps the door shut.*

L-Cpl Finnigan (*off*)   Open up, open up!

Thunder and lightning.

Ellen *and* **Dermot** *struggle.*

Dermot   Jesus save us, Ellen! Ellen, please!

Ellen   Stay back, I said!

Dermot   Don't fight with me, not now!

Ellen (*breaks free*)   Stay back, stay back! Mammy, please, they're here!

Ellen *rushes to* **Maryanne** *and tries to wake her.*

Dermot *holds the cabin door shut, as* **L-Cpl Finnigan** *continues to boot it down.*

Ellen   The soldiers have come for us – look! Wake up, Mammy, please!

L-Cpl Finnigan (*off*)   Open the door, you fucking weasel!

Ellen   Won't you live to see our freedom?! I'm telling you, they're –

L-Cpl Finnigan *boots down the door, and enters.*

Ellen   – here, look, they're here!

Dermot (*tries to flee from* **Finnigan**)   You'll not touch me, you beast!

L-Cpl Finnigan (*grabs* **Dermot**)   What, do you go by fucking Abraham or something?!

Dermot   I'm warning you, don't . . . !

L-Cpl Finnigan   That you should escape your own judgement!

Dermot *draws his blade from his pocket.*

L-Cpl Finnigan   That you think you can get past me with your –

Dermot *stabs* **L-Cpl Finnigan** *with his knife.*

Pause.

L-Cpl Finnigan   Oh Jesus, no.

Dermot *stabs* **L-Cpl Finnigan** *twice.*

Pause.

L-Cpl Finnigan   Oh Lucy . . .

Dermot *stabs* **L-Cpl Finnigan** *several more times.*

He falls to the ground.

Thunder and lightning.

Long pause.

Ellen   Dermot –

Dermot   Be silent, Ellen, damn you!

Ellen   But –

Dermot   Silence, I say!

He throws his blade to the ground.

Long pause.

Ellen   But he came to take us away.

Pause.

Dirty murdering –

Dermot   Oh, that's right, Ellen, that's right, you give me that title!

Ellen (*makes for* **Finnigan**)   But he was one of Daddy's friends!

Dermot *bars* **Ellen** *from the dead body, grabbing her. They struggle.*

Dermot   Aye, friend, that's right, and may the flies hatch their eggs in his wound! A thousand filthy maggots, so be it! Might they hatch in his mouth and wriggle their way out through his hole! I'll take any number of them, you hear?! I'll take God Himself so help me!

Ellen   Stop it, I say – let go!

Ellen *breaks free from* **Dermot**, *darting back to* **Maryanne**.

Dermot   That's right, you run right back to her now!

Ellen   You're not in your right mind!

Dermot   Run back to that hag, go on! Go on with you!

Ellen   Dermot, please . . .

Dermot   She who would fail her own son!

Ellen   But that's not it at all!

Dermot   She who would send me to my grave! Who would betray her own word!

Ellen   No, you're wrong!

Dermot   The storm's in her pocket, Ellen, do you think I don't know that?!

Ellen *tends to* **Maryanne**.

Long pause.

Dermot   She's turned the town against itself, look.

Long pause.

Ellen, please, we have to believe that.

Long pause.

We have to believe something.

Long pause.

Look at me.

Ellen   No . . .

Dermot   Let us believe something. Anything . . .

Ellen   God is with us always, Dermot.

Dermot   God would never do this to His own kind.

Pause.

Well, would he?

Thunder and lightning.

Long pause.

Come on now, sister, do my words mean nothing to you any more?

Long pause.

Ellen, please . . .

Ellen   Let me fasten your chains at least.

Dermot   Am I not your brother?

Ellen   We can fasten your chains, Dermot, come on!

She removes a padlock and key from **Maryanne**'*s pocket.*

Pause.

Ellen   For your own protection.

Dermot   Oh . . .

Ellen   Come on now, please.

Dermot   We can, can't we?

Ellen   Let me help you back to the tree.

Dermot   We can do that, Ellen, you traitor!

Ellen   Please, just –

Dermot   We can do just as Mammy says!

Ellen   Just stop being so stupid, you know it's for your own good.

Dermot   We can fall on our knees and grovel!

Ellen   You don't want another murder on your hands.

Dermot   Might we do that, sister?

Ellen   Look . . .

Dermot   What else might we do? Well, come on!

Ellen   I'm only trying to help . . .

Dermot   Might I be chained to the oak for Mammy to beat me?

Ellen   But we can be a family again.

Dermot   What, to keep me as a slave to serve her supper? To fetch in wood and keep the vermin at bay? Might I do that, Ellen?

He wrestles the padlock and key from **Ellen**.

Dermot   Might I take your stinking key and bind myself at your command?

Ellen   Dermot, please!

Dermot   Might I do that?

Ellen   You're not allowed to do that, don't break the rules.

Dermot   Here!

He moves to the post – a tree that forms part of the cabin – and fastens himself to it with the padlock and key.

Let me help you, Ellen, please!

Thunder and lightning.

Let me serve at your command – here I am! Here I am, Ellen! Tied to the post as you bid!

He pulls himself to his feet with difficulty.

Well? What would you have me do, oh Queen? What else would you have me do?

Ellen *returns to* **Maryanne**, *crouching down by her.*

Long pause.

Dermot   What else, Ellen?

Ellen   No.

Dermot   What else?

Ellen   You're not being very fair, Dermot.

Dermot   I'm here for you – look.

Ellen   We can't carry on like this.

Dermot   I'm here for you, Ellen, come on. That I should pay for your sins. That Mammy should make me suffer.

Ellen   We must pray like good girls and boys.

Dermot   Ellen, please! I can choose this madness no longer! What, should I lay down my life to you?! Should I give you my flesh?! My hands and my feet, my nose and my throat! These two pitiful fucking jellies?! Shall I offer them up for you now?!

He clutches his eyeballs with both hands.

Oh, that the earth would swallow me whole! That I would —

He claws and drags the eyes from out of his head.

– never have have been your witness!!

Thunder and lightning.

Long pause.

He kneels on the ground, blinded.

Long pause.

Cpl O'Connor *and* **Lieut Ryan**, *swords drawn, silently enter the cabin, unnoticed by the children.*

Lieut Ryan *moves straight to the body of* **L-Cpl Finnigan** *and crouches down by him.*

Cpl O'Connor *moves to* **Ellen** *and takes her hand.*

Long pause.

Dermot   Ellen.

Cpl O'Connor *leads* **Ellen** *out of the cabin. They exit.*

Lieut Ryan *tries to resuscitate* **L-Cpl Finnigan**.

Maryanne *is beginning to regain consciousness, pulling herself onto all fours.*

Long pause.

Dermot   Ellen.

Pause.

Look on me, girl.

Long pause.

Ellen . . .

Maryanne (*barely conscious*)   You're a good boy, Dermot.

Dermot (*to* **Ellen**)   Won't you look on me?

Maryanne *begins to crawl towards* **Dermot**, *very slowly.*

Long pause.

Dermot   Won't you tell me what to do?

Long pause.

Who else can we tell but each other?

Maryanne *has crawled over to* **Dermot** *and begins undoing his chains.*

Long pause.

Dermot   Ellen, please, I'm begging you!

Lieut Ryan *clubs* **Maryanne** *over the head with the butt of his sword.*

Dermot   Tell me what to do!

Blackout.

Five

Night.

The storm continues outside, clearly audible.

Col Fleming's *quarters – austere and elegant, candlelit.*

Col Fleming, *an Englishman, is sitting at his desk, slowly reading through a parchment.*

Lieut Coyle, *battered and bruised, stands at a distance before* **Col Fleming**. *In front of* **Lieut Coyle** *is an empty chair.*

Sgt Browne, **Capt Farrell** *and* **Capt Skelton** *stand in a line, behind* **Col Fleming**.

Col Fleming   What should we do with him?

Lieut Coyle   I couldn't say, sir.

Long pause.

Col Fleming   Are you uncomfortable?

Long pause.

Lieutenant Coyle . . .

Lieut Coyle   I don't think I understand the question, sir.

Col Fleming   You're hard of hearing?

Lieut Coyle   No, Colonel, I . . .

Col Fleming   Should I raise my voice for you?

Lieut Coyle   Uncomfortable.

Col Fleming   What?

Lieut Coyle   A little, sir, yes.

Pause.

The boys were somewhat rough with me, I'd say.

Col Fleming   They were.

Lieut Coyle   Yes . . .

Col Fleming   That's understandable.

Lieut Coyle   Yes, sir.

Pause.

Perfectly.

Col Fleming   What?

Lieut Coyle   They were . . .

Col Fleming   Your boys are grieving for their homeland, are they not?

Lieut Coyle   Yes.

Pause.

Yes, possibly . . .

Col Fleming   Am I hearing things, Sergeant Browne?

Sgt Browne   A mutter, Colonel.

Col Fleming   Oh.

Sgt Browne   I believe the Lieutenant muttered something.

Col Fleming   I see.

Sgt Browne   Under his breath.

Lieut Coyle   They had good reason, sir.

Col Fleming   Thank you, Sergeant.

Lieut Coyle   They were perfectly within their rights, I mean.

Col Fleming   Yes.

Lieut Coyle   Colonel, please –

Col Fleming   Yes, that's –

Lieut Coyle   If you would just let me explain –

Col Fleming   That's much more like it, Coyle, but you don't have to shout the whole house down.

He continues reading the parchment.

Long pause.

You were recruited at eighteen.

Lieut Coyle   Yes, sir.

Col Fleming   Though you come from a Catholic family.

Lieut Coyle   Well . . .

Col Fleming   It says here your brother was executed.

Lieut Coyle   That's correct, yes.

Pause.

A fortnight after your arrival, sir.

Pause.

He bought a horse for over five pounds.

Col Fleming   He was a farmer.

Lieut Coyle   Yes.

Col Fleming   He and his wife owned . . .

Lieut Coyle   The farm you've occupied these past twenty years, Colonel, yes.

Col Fleming   A man of property, yes?

Lieut Coyle   Moderate, yes, I suppose.

Col Fleming   How very interesting.

Long pause.

Lieut Coyle   Colonel, please, if you think that I had any hand –

Col Fleming   It doesn't seem particularly fair, though.

Lieut Coyle   Sir.

Col Fleming   To take a man's life for the sale of a horse.

Lieut Coyle   I don't –

Col Fleming   Is that fair?

Lieut Coyle   He broke the law, sir.

Col Fleming   So it would seem.

Pause.

And his wife?

Lieut Coyle   Yes, sir.

Col Fleming   You bore her children.

Lieut Coyle   Every man has his vice, sir.

Col Fleming   Well said.

Pause.

Lieut Coyle   Forgive me, but . . .

Col Fleming   There are certain pleasures your own wife cannot give, yes?

Lieut Coyle   Well . . .

Col Fleming   The curse of familiarity.

Lieut Coyle   As much as any man.

Col Fleming   Though you have married into considerable wealth.

Lieut Coyle   I do not doubt her charity, sir.

Col Fleming   I know her family well.

Lieut Coyle   They speak highly of you, sir.

Col Fleming   Munitions.

Lieut Coyle   That's right, yes.

Col Fleming   And you would jeopardise this wealth?

Long pause.

Are you unhappy, Lieutenant?

Lieut Coyle   Possibly, sir.

Col Fleming   Just 'possibly'?

Lieut Coyle   Yes. Yes, I mean . . .

Col Fleming   I'm surprised you're not hanging from one of our trees.

Lieut Coyle   I am your servant, sir.

Col Fleming   I dare say you could lose some weight. Are you fit enough to go into war, do you think?

Lieut Coyle   Oh . . .

Col Fleming   One very much doubts it.

Lieut Coyle   Yes, sir, of course.

Col Fleming   We leave in two days' time, I –

Lieut Coyle   Irrefutably, Your Honour.

Col Fleming   What?

Lieut Coyle   Of course, I mean –

Col Fleming   Speak up, Lieutenant!

Lieut Coyle (*salutes*)   For His Majesty the King, sir, yes!

Long pause.

Lieut Coyle *remains saluting while* **Col Fleming** *again returns to the parchment.*

Long pause.

Col Fleming   Perhaps you need time to rest.

Long pause.

Perhaps we've expected too much from you.

Lieut Coyle   I don't know what you mean . . .

Col Fleming   As you were. Lieutenant.

Lieut Coyle (*salutes*)   Sir!

Long pause.

Col Fleming   What do you say, Captain?

Capt Farrell   I would post his head to London.

Long pause.

Col Fleming   Skelton?

Capt Skelton   On a pike, sir, yes.

Col Fleming   Though I would very much like to meet this family of his.

Long pause.

You do then know the penalty for sedition?

Lieut Coyle   Yes, Your Honour, I do.

Col Fleming   Yet you feel responsible for this man.

Lieut Coyle   He is my son, sir.

Col Fleming   Under the authority of Rome.

Pause.

Lieut Coyle   Colonel, please, you must know –

Col Fleming (*to* **Farrell**)   Do we have a confession yet, Farrell?

Capt Farrell   I have it with me here, sir.

Lieut Coyle   The boy didn't know what he was doing.

Capt Farrell *passes* **Col Fleming** *a scroll.*

Lieut Coyle   He needs a doctor, that's all, sir, he's . . .

Col Fleming *reads the scroll.*

Lieut Coyle   He's not in his right mind, I . . .

Pause.

He was drunk, sir, he'd say anything to –

Col Fleming   You are of course entitled to appeal on his behalf.

He passes the scroll to **Capt Farrell**, *who then passes it to* **Lieut Coyle**.

Capt Farrell *moves back to his post while* **Lieut Coyle** *reads the parchment.*

Long pause.

Lieut Coyle   Of course, sir, yes.

Col Fleming   Although you would have to stand trial yourself.

Long pause.

Perhaps you sympathise with these people.

Long pause.

Perhaps you think we have no place in this country of yours.

Long pause.

Civilisation is a process, Lieutenant. It can take years. Generations even. I doubt our own grandchildren will live to see the fulfilment of our project. What we do here has repercussions that go beyond anything you or I can imagine. After all, you've proved you're quite capable of adopting our language. I'm equally sure you can assist in the reformation of your parliament when the time comes. But as you people seem unable to rise above the so-called inequalities of the past, our presence here should remain intact, should it not?

Lieut Coyle   Yes, sir.

Col Fleming   Yours is a nation bred for slavery.

Lieut Coyle   Yes, I see.

Col Fleming   It sits at the very roots of your culture. You excel at it.

Lieut Coyle   Thank you.

Col Fleming   St Patrick was an Englishman, Lieutenant.

Pause.

Well?

Long pause.

I had hoped you would have embraced the benefits of service by now. You're quite an inspiration to the men.

Lieut Coyle   It is an honour, of course.

Col Fleming   What should we do with him?

Blackout.

Six

The mud cabin.

Night.

A storm – thunder, lightning and heavy rain.

Maryanne *is sitting on the stool by the peat fire, her back to* **Col Fleming**. *Her face is scarred.*

Col Fleming *is sitting on the edge of the bed, semi-naked. His back and face are scratched, and his wig is removed.*

Lieut Coyle *and* **Lieut Ryan** *guard the cabin door.*

Long pause.

Maryanne   Was everything to your satisfaction, sir?

Long pause.

You're not frightened of the thunder, I hope?

Long pause.

Colonel Fleming, sir . . .

Col Fleming   I'm fine.

Maryanne   Oh.

Pause.

Oh, then maybe your men here would –

Col Fleming   Be quiet.

Maryanne   Yes, sir.

Pause.

Of course, sir.

Long pause.

She lays peat on the fire.

Col Fleming *reaches for his uniform.*

Pause.

He reaches into the pocket of his uniform and removes a drinking flask.

He unscrews the top and takes a drink.

Pause.

He goes to take a second drink.

Maryanne   There's to be quite the storm, I feel.

Col Fleming   There is.

Maryanne   You should feel the way it batters against this old door. You'd think the four horsemen were trying to break in. You'd think the very earth was split in two.

Col Fleming   I can't say I ever pitied a door before.

Maryanne   She is terrified of the thunder. The girl. I mean. She thinks it's out to get her. The thunder and lightning. she thinks it's holding a grudge somehow.

Col Fleming   It can be quite frightening. I imagine.

Maryanne   Well. I don't know where she gets it.

Col Fleming   No.

Maryanne   Though we can none of us hold our fears to ransom, can we, sir?

Pause.

It was spiders with me. Do you like spiders?

Col Fleming   Not particularly.

Maryanne   Do you need more time. sir?

Col Fleming   What?

Maryanne   Would you like me to go back outside?

Long pause.

Maryanne *hands* **Col Fleming** *his wig from the floor. He puts the wig on and takes a drink from the flask.*

Long pause.

Maryanne   I pity that poor horse of yours, Colonel. It can't be good for her, left stranded out there in the cold.

Col Fleming   He should manage, miss.

Maryanne   Would you like me to take him a small blanket?

Pause.

Not that it would provide him much shelter, of course. There's little mercy spared for these hills, sir. There's little life left at all.

Col Fleming   I'm sorry to hear that.

Maryanne   There hasn't one leaf grown from this tree since I last cared remember. I haven't seen so much as a rabbit in years. Not even a priest.

Col Fleming   A pity.

Maryanne   Not a Jesuit, sir, no. They'd sooner brave hanging.

Pause.

Maryanne   They'd sooner brave the lamb, sir.

Long pause.

Will you be riding back to town tonight?

Col Fleming   I expect so, yes.

Maryanne   I could take it off your bill.

Col Fleming   What?

Maryanne   The thunder and lightning.

Pause.

If it's disturbed you, that is.

Long pause.

Although I don't mean to suggest . . .

Col Fleming   That's very kind of you, miss.

Maryanne   I hope you don't think it too forward of me.

Col Fleming   You're not forward.

Maryanne   You were gone an awful long time.

Pause.

You were gone a good while, sir, yes.

Long pause.

Would you like me to clean your wounds for you?

Col Fleming   I'm sorry?

Maryanne   You're bleeding, sir.

Col Fleming   Oh . . .

Maryanne   I might clean your wounds for you.

Long pause.

She remained courteous, I hope.

Long pause.

She remained courteous . . .

Col Fleming   Yes.

Maryanne   Are you sure you're not too cold? I could always lay more turf on the fire.

Pause.

It's no trouble, sir . . .

Col Fleming   Here.

Maryanne   What?

Col Fleming   Take it.

Col Fleming *offers* **Maryanne** *his flask.*

Maryanne   Oh . . .

Col Fleming   Take it.

Maryanne   Oh no, Your Honour, I didn't mean –

Col Fleming   Go on.

Pause.

Maryanne *takes the flask.*

Maryanne   May God protect you, sir.

She drinks from the flask.

Pause.

She goes to hand the flask back . . .

She takes a drink from the flask.

Pause.

She hesitates.

Pause.

She hands the flask back to **Col Fleming**.

Maryanne   Thank you, Colonel.

Pause.

Colonel Fleming, sir . . .

Col Fleming   Forgive me.

Maryanne   What?

Col Fleming   Forgive me.

Long pause.

Maryanne   Well, that is very decent of you, sir, thank you.

She pockets the flask of whisky.

Long pause.

Dead pig, sir.

Col Fleming   Sorry?

Maryanne   Dead pig.

Pause.

A little bacon, sir.

Col Fleming   Thank you, no.

Pause.

Maryanne   Oh well then, maybe . . .

Col Fleming   It is custom for the servant to dress her master.

Maryanne   It is?

Pause.

Oh . . .

Col Fleming   I thought you'd be accustomed to such duties.

Maryanne   Oh, yes . . .

Col Fleming   If you're concerned with payment . . .

Maryanne   Oh, good God . . .

Col Fleming   I am an honourable man . . .

Maryanne   Maryanne, sir.

Col Fleming   . . . Maryanne.

Maryanne   Might you care to stand up?

Pause.

Col Fleming *stands up.*

Long pause.

Maryanne (*remains seated*)   I'm sure she won't be long now, sir.

Long pause.

Maryanne   Ellen.

Pause.

Ellen.

Long pause.

Come on now, Ellen.

She moves to the head of the bed.

Come on now, Ellen, the Colonel's waiting for you.

She peers under the blankets on the bed.

Long pause.

She replaces the blankets.

Long pause.

She begins to silently dress **Col Fleming**.

Long pause.

Lieut Ryan *moves to the corner of the cabin and takes a shovel that is propped up against the wall.*

Lieut Ryan *offers the shovel to* **Lieut Coyle**.

Lieut Ryan   Well, go on.

Pause.

Take it, Lieutenant.

Lieut Coyle   Yes, sir.

Pause.

He takes the shovel.

Lieut Ryan *returns to guard the cabin door.*

Pause.

Lieut Coyle *finds a suitable space on the cabin floor. He begins digging a hole in the cabin floor.*

Maryanne *dresses* **Col Fleming** *and* **Lieut Coyle** *digs the hole.*

Long pause.

Maryanne   Will you be sailing tomorrow morning, sir?

Col Fleming   That's right.

Maryanne   You must be looking forward to seeing your family.

Col Fleming   Yes.

Maryanne   Not that we . . .

Pause.

Begging your pardon, sir.

Col Fleming   Go on.

Maryanne   We will all be sorry to see you go, of course.

Pause.

She continues dressing **Col Fleming**.

Maryanne   Will you be sailing to Europe with your regiment?

Col Fleming   Of course.

Maryanne   Then I shall pray for you, sir.

Long pause.

She finishes dressing **Col Fleming**, *apart from his boots. He moves to the stool by the fire and sits down.*

Pause.

Maryanne *takes the boots from by the fire, then kneels down before* **Col Fleming**.

Pause.

She begins to put the boots on **Col Fleming**.

Col Fleming   You have a very beautiful country.

Maryanne (*stops*)   Sorry, sir?

Col Fleming   The land.

Maryanne   Oh . . .

Col Fleming   You have very beautiful land.

Maryanne   Oh, we do.

Col Fleming   I shall miss the long walks.

Maryanne   We shall miss you, sir.

Pause.

Maryanne *proceeds to put* **Col Fleming**'s *boots on.*

As she does this, **Lieut Coyle** *finishes digging the hole.*

He moves over to the small makeshift bed and pulls back the blankets. He picks up and carries **Ellen**'s *body to the hole. He lays* **Ellen**'s *body in the hole.*

Pause.

Lieut Coyle *begins burying* **Ellen** *as* **Maryanne** *finishes with* **Col Fleming**'s *boots.*

Long pause.

Maryanne   Will that be all, Colonel?

Col Fleming   That's all.

Maryanne   Are they tight enough for you?

Col Fleming   Thank you.

Maryanne *remains kneeling.*

Long pause.

Maryanne (*goes to stand*)   Well . . .

Col Fleming   Oh.

Maryanne (*kneels*)   Yes, sir.

Col Fleming   My debt.

Pause.

He takes the purse from his uniform. He counts a small number of coins from the purse, and hands them to **Maryanne**.

Col Fleming   You may want to count it.

Maryanne *counts the coins.*

Pause.

Maryanne   Thank you, Colonel.

Lieut Coyle *continues burying* **Ellen**.

Long pause.

Maryanne   If there's anything more I can do.

Long pause.

If there's anything you need for your journey, sir.

Long pause.

If I might offer my service.

Pause.

If you're in need of a servant.

Col Fleming   I might.

Maryanne   For the voyage ahead, I mean.

Pause.

Forgive me if I'm being too forward.

Long pause.

Col Fleming   Do you renounce your Pope?

Maryanne   I spit on his cunt.

Long pause.

Him and all his high priests.

Col Fleming   I trust you don't mean . . .

Maryanne   Jesus Christ, sir.

Col Fleming   Oh.

Pause.

Maryanne   Redemption is a lie told by writers and bureaucrats. There are those that lean out the pulpit, and they may speak awful sweet. The life to be. Of epiphany and liberation. But they're no different to them that stand in office. Offering hope when it's truth what's needed. Truth being no more than murder.

Col Fleming   I see.

Maryanne   He can rot in the earth with the rest of us.

Long pause.

The only virtue I crave, sir, is constancy.

Long pause.

Maryanne *offers* **Col Fleming** *his gloves from by the fire.*

Maryanne   You might sell me your horse.

Col Fleming   What?

Maryanne   You might sell me your horse.

Col Fleming *takes his gloves.*

Pause.

Maryanne   You might do that, sir.

Col Fleming   I might.

Maryanne   You could do that for me, sir, yes.

Col Fleming *sits on the stool as he puts on his gloves.*

Maryanne *remains kneeling.*

Long pause.

Col Fleming   Go on.

Maryanne   You could buy back my cattle.

Long pause.

My farm. You could buy back my farm.

Long pause.

What else could you do for me, Colonel?

Lieut Coyle *continues burying* **Ellen.**

Maryanne   What else? Tell me. What else?

Blackout.

Seven

Dawn.

The storm receding: heavy rain, turning light, and the sun slowly rising.

The patch of grassland, before the town gates.

Dermot *is in the stocks.*

Ellen *is sitting on the grass, a distance apart from* **Dermot***.*

The **Fiddler** *and the* **Piper** *sit on the grass, a distance apart from them both.*

Long pause.

Ellen   A dozen eyes, you say?

Dermot   A dozen.

Ellen   Oh.

Dermot   A dozen dozen.

Ellen   That's just terrible, isn't it?

Long pause.

Dermot   Did you see him?

Pause.

Ellen.

Pause.

You saw him, didn't you, girl?

Long pause.

Ellen . . .

Ellen   Great long fangs he has.

Dermot   What?

Ellen   Great huge fangs.

Dermot   No!

Ellen   Snarling and foaming like a bear. Wielding his sword.

Dermot   One from every other hand. Calling on my submission, the brute.

Ellen   That's right, Dermot, yes.

Dermot   To think he could do this to his own kind.

Ellen   Oh, he was a terrible-sounding Devil all right.

Dermot   Didn't I tell you, Ellen?

Pause.

I told you, didn't I?

Ellen   Oh, yes . . .

Dermot   Then you must've been scared to death.

Ellen   Yes, I was.

Dermot   I know I would.

Long pause.

Dermot   Ellen . . .

Ellen   Of course, I told him you were sleeping.

Dermot   Did you?

Ellen   He's not to be disturbed, I said. 'Don't you be bothering him, you old bastard!'

Dermot   You didn't!

Ellen   'You leave him alone, you cruel beast! Get down under the earth where you belong! Get down, I tell you, don't you be bothering my brother!'

Long pause.

That'll teach him, won't it?

Dermot   It will.

Ellen   That'll teach him.

Dermot   You're a good girl, Ellen.

Long pause.

The **Fiddler** *and* **Piper** *begin to play a hymn as the sun rises.*

Long pause.

Dermot   Ellen . . .

Ellen   Quiet now, that's enough.

Pause.

Ellen *stands and moves over to* **Dermot**.

She removes a hunk of bread from her pocket.

She climbs onto the small stool by the stocks.

She tears a piece of bread from the hunk and feeds it to **Dermot***.*

Long pause.

Ellen   Of course, it'll all turn right in the end.

Long pause.

It'll all turn right, Dermot, yes.

Dermot   Will it?

Ellen   Of course.

Dermot   Oh . . .

Ellen   Yes, of course it will, don't be silly.

She climbs down off the stool. She takes her cloth and bucket and washes **Dermot***.*

Long pause.

Ellen   You might grant me that, no?

Pause.

Ellen   Dermot . . .

Dermot   It'll all turn right, Ellen.

Ellen   Daddy promised to speak to the man.

Dermot   Who?

Ellen   The good man.

Dermot   You mean Jesus.

Ellen   No, stupid. The English-speaking man.

Dermot   Was Jesus not English?

Ellen   The man takes care of Daddy, you know. The man who's going to take us away.

Dermot   Where?

Ellen   On the boat of course.

Dermot   Oh.

Ellen   The boat sailing for England.

Long pause.

You remember, don't you, Dermot?

Long pause.

Dermot . . .

Dermot   I remember, child.

Ellen   You believe me though, don't you?

Ellen *rinses the blood from the cloth into the bucket.*

Long pause.

And then we'll be all right, you'll see.

Pause.

And then we'll be free.

Lights fade.

Faces in the Crowd

Faces in the Crowd was first performed at the Royal Court Jerwood Theatre Upstairs, London, on 18 October 2008 with the following cast and creative team:

Joanne   Amanda Drew
Dave   Con O'Neill

Director Clare Lizzimore
Designers William Fricker, Rae Smith
Lighting Designer Johanna Town
Sound Designer Emma Laxton
Casting Director Amy Ball
Production Manager Tariq Sayyid Rifaat
Costume Supervisor Jackie Orton
Voice Coach Sally Hague

Characters

Dave, *forty-four years old*
Joanne, *thirty-nine years old*

Both are originally from Sheffield, South Yorkshire.

Setting

Dave's studio flat, east London.

The building is situated in Shoreditch, sandwiched between Bishopsgate, Hoxton and Bethnal Green.

The building is made up of offices on the ground floor and, above them, three studio flats.

Dave's flat is the middle one – Flat B.

The flat comprises three separate spaces:

> The living space, which includes: a kitchen area (counter/stools/ cooker/hob/cupboards/fridge); an office area (desk/laptop/files/ junk) by the window (with blinds); and, in the centre, a 'living area' including a futon, a plasma-screen TV and a small armchair.

> The bathroom (toilet, sink, cabinet, bath/shower unit).

> The bedroom. Like the living space, the bedroom has its own window (with blinds), looking out onto the street below and the ex-council flats opposite. There is a king-size bed, a bedside cabinet, a chest of drawers, etc.

Three doors.

The rest of the furniture and interior decoration is made obvious in the text.

Studio flat, east London.

Summer 2007. Night.

The windows and blinds are shut.

Dave *is with* **Joanne**.

Joanne *has just arrived, standing close by the door. She carries her large brown handbag and wears casual clothes.*

Dave *is in his work suit.*

Long pause.

Dave   Did yer find it alright?

Joanne   Just about.

Pause.

Dave   Sorry.

Joanne   What?

Dave   Should've come and met yer shunt I? Off the tube, I mean.

Joanne   It weren't far.

Dave   No, but . . .

Pause.

This area.

Joanne   Yeah, I noticed.

Dave   Not as bad as it looks.

Joanne   Int it?

Dave   There's people spend a fortune to live round 'ere. Yer could buy a three-bedroom house back home f'what yer'd pay for one of these.

Joanne   That's London for yer then int it?

Dave   Yeah.

Pause.

Yeah it is.

Joanne   I like it.

Dave   D'yer?

Joanne   It's nice.

Dave   Oh . . .

Joanne   Self-contained.

Dave   Oh, well . . .

Joanne   Better than I expected anyway.

Dave   Thanks.

Over the following, **Joanne** *snoops round the flat.*

Long pause.

Joanne   Don't mind me havin' a nose d'yer?

Long pause.

This all yours?

Dave   What?

Joanne   The furniture. This all your doin'?

Dave   Partly.

Joanne   I see.

Dave   He owns the whole building.

Joanne   Who?

Dave   The landlord. I work with 'is brother.

Joanne   Oh, right.

Dave   We've become sort of friends. On and off. At work, I mean. It's him who put us on to this.

Joanne   Good of 'im.

Dave   It's only temporary. He's away with the navy. Marcus. I mean – that's the landlord. He's stationed down Southampton f'the rest of the year.

Joanne   Landed on yer feet then 'ant yer?

Dave   Well, it'll do like.

Joanne   Minimalist.

Pause.

That is what they call it, isn't it?

Dave   I wunt know, Joanne.

Joanne   Looks smaller from the outside.

Dave   Tardis.

Joanne   What?

Dave   Doctor Who's Tardis. That's what we call it.

Pause.

Yeah.

Long pause.

Though I was thinkin' of movin' further into Hackney.

Pause.

Further in . . .

Joanne   This the bathroom through 'ere?

Dave   Oh . . .

Joanne *opens the bathroom door and peers in.*

Dave   Yeah. Yeah, that's . . .

Joanne   Smells clean.

Dave   Thanks.

Joanne   Someone's got 'im trained.

Dave   I wouldn't go that far.

Joanne   Wunt yer?

Dave   I wouldn't, no.

Joanne *switches the light on and steps inside.*

Pause.

Joanne   D'yer mind if I . . . ?

Dave   No, you . . .

Joanne *shuts the bathroom door.*

Dave   Don't mind me.

Long pause.

Joanne *goes to the toilet.*

Once finished, she flushes and moves to the bathroom sink.

She washes her hands, filling up the sink with water.

Pause.

Joanne *proceeds to wash her face, washing her make-up off.*

Once done, she dries her face with a towel and checks her reflection.

She opens the bathroom cabinet and snoops around inside.

She examines, among other things, a box of tampons, and a tube of Canesten cream.

As she is doing all this, **Dave***, in the other room, hesitates.*

Pause.

Dave *moves to the kitchen area, removes a bottle of white wine from the fridge and takes two wine glasses from the cupboard.*

He is about to open the bottle of wine when his mobile phone starts ringing.

He rushes to find the mobile phone.

He finds the mobile phone, which is in the pocket of his suit jacket, draped over one of the kitchen stools.

He takes the mobile phone, presses the 'busy' button.

The mobile phone stops ringing.

He turns the mobile phone onto silent, then pockets it.

He hesitates.

Pause.

He moves to the window.

He looks out of the window.

He shuts the window and pulls the blinds down.

He unbuttons the top button of his shirt.

He turns the fan on.

He hesitates.

Pause.

He takes the mobile phone out of his pocket.

He presses a couple of buttons, then puts the phone to his ear and listens to a voice message.

As he listens, he tidies up the papers on his work desk.

He then spots a pair of tracksuit bottoms and a T-shirt on the futon.

He grabs them both and looks for somewhere to put them.

He turns off the mobile phone and puts it in his pocket.

He enters the bedroom, and throws the tracksuit bottoms and T-shirt under the bed.

He re-enters the central living space.

Joanne *re-enters, turning the bathroom light off and shutting the door.*

Joanne   Cosy.

Dave   Well, like I say . . .

Joanne   Yer lookin' after it for 'im.

Dave   It's not cheap.

Joanne   It doesn't look cheap.

Dave   Should've seen the dump I was in before.

Over the next, **Joanne** *makes herself at home. She moves to the kitchen area and puts her handbag down on one of the chairs. She takes her cigarettes from her jacket, then takes her jacket off, draping it over one of the stools. She sits on the stool.*

Dave *follows her to the kitchen area and proceeds to open the bottle of wine and pour two glasses.*

Dave   Over the river, over in Peckham. This is what, comin' up five year back now? Used t' take me about two hours just t' get to n' from work every day.

Joanne   Must've took its toll.

Dave   Bloody shoebox.

Joanne   Weren't yer knackered?

Dave   That's what I mean.

Joanne   I'm knackered just gettin' through King's Cross in one piece.

Dave   Good journey was it?

Joanne   What?

Dave   The train.

Joanne   I suppose so, yeah.

Dave   Yer weren't held up or anything?

Joanne   Straight through.

Dave   That's good then int it?

Joanne   Stopped once at Chesterfield. Once again at Leicester.

Dave   Good, yeah.

Joanne   Luton then 'ere.

Dave   Right.

Joanne   St Pancras.

Dave   No, that's good, Joanne.

Joanne   Tube all the way to Old Street.

Dave   Beats the bloody coach dunt it?

Joanne   By about four hour, yeah.

She sparks a cigarette.

Long pause.

Yer accent's gone.

Dave   Has it?

Joanne   Yer don't sound like you.

Long pause.

Dave *opens one of the cupboards and fetches* **Joanne** *an ashtray, which he places on the side.*

Dave   I was livin' in Plumstead before then. Before Peckham, that is.

Joanne   Where?

Dave   House share. Me n' a bunch of ex-grads. Fuckin' . . .

He hands **Joanne** *her glass of wine.*

Pause.

Dave   Yeah.

Joanne   Moved about a bit then, yeah?

Dave   'Ere n' there. Yer know. Get me bearings.

Joanne   Took its toll I see.

Dave   What?

Joanne   No wonder yer goin' bald.

Dave   Bald?

Joanne   Thought I'd got the wrong address for a minute.

Pause.

Dave   Oh . . .

Joanne   I'm jokin', yer prat, can't yer take a joke?

With her wine and cigarette, she moves to the window and peers through the blinds.

Long pause.

View's not up to much.

Dave   Sorry?

Joanne   Can't say it's too inspiring. The Texaco.

Dave   Yer can see the Gherkin during the day.

Joanne   I can see the what?

Dave   The Gherkin, yer know? Norman Foster.

Joanne   Weren't too taken wi' the homeless either. D'they always look like that?

Dave   Like what?

Joanne   Like they just stepped out o' Topshop.

Dave   'Ow d'yer mean?

Joanne   Bit trendy aren't they?

Dave   Are they?

Joanne   Brand-new pair o' trainers on the tramp.

Dave   'Oo?

Joanne   Beardy bollocks by the cashpoint there. 'Im n' 'is Alsation.

Dave   Yeah, he's always . . .

Pause.

He's somethin' of a fixture . . . –

Joanne   Gi'im a shave yer could stick 'im on a catwalk.

Dave   'Im or the dog?

Joanne   'E could give you a run f'yer money. (*Of* **Dave**'s *shirt.*) What is that, Sainsbury's own?

Dave   Fuck off, it's Paul Smith.

Joanne   I'm surprised yer can put up with that noise.

Pause.

No offence.

Dave   None taken.

Joanne   Someone as sensitive as you. Thought yer'd be livin' in the woods or somert.

She moves to the office area and sits at **Dave**'s *desk, peering at the laptop screen and his papers.*

Pause.

Joanne   I've got me own business now.

Dave   Okay.

Joanne   I've got me own little florist's, Dave, yeah.

Dave   Oh, right.

Joanne *digs in her pocket and pulls out a business card, which she offers to* **Dave**, *who takes it.*

Joanne   Found a place up in Woodseats goin' f'sale. This is, what? Eighteen month back. Used t' be a kiddies' clothes shop.

Dave   Brilliant.

Joanne   It's me dad's doin' really. 'E stripped it all out, 'im n' our Phillip.

Dave   That's good of 'im.

Joanne   Well 'e's hardly goin' t' say no.

Dave   I always liked your brother.

Joanne   Mum's been helpin' out with all the day-to-day . . . yer know?

Dave   Doin' well f'yerself then, yeah?

Joanne   We're doin' alright, Dave, yeah. All things considerin'. Valentines, weddings, the odd funeral 'ere n' there.

Dave   Cashin' in on the dead.

Joanne   Got t' pay yer way somehow.

Dave   Got to, yeah.

Pause.

He offers the business card back to **Joanne**, *who takes it.*

Dave   I like the little bumblebees.

Joanne   Are you plannin' on goin' to Borneo?

Dave   Why would I want to go to Borneo?

Joanne   That's what it says here.

Dave   No, I'm . . . –

Joanne   The Orangutan Conservation Project.

Dave   I was just browsing a few sites, that's all.

Joanne   That's very noble of yer, Dave.

Dave   It's fascinatin' stuff really.

Joanne   Aren't they payin' you enough at that firm o' yours?

Dave   They're payin' me fine.

Joanne   Can't 'ave got much job satisfaction then can yer?

She enters the bedroom, turning the light on.

Long pause.

She snoops round the bedroom.

Dave *puts his wine down and moves out of the kitchen area.*

He goes to the laptop. Unseen by **Joanne***, he saves and shuts down a program and half closes the laptop lid.*

Joanne *sits on the bed, snooping at the bits and pieces on the bedside table.*

Dave *retrieves his glass of wine and then moves to the bedroom, standing in the doorway.*

Long pause.

Dave   Yeah, that's . . . –

Joanne   Impressive.

Dave   Yeah.

Joanne   King size.

Dave   It's not mine.

Joanne   Int it?

Dave   No, it's . . . —

Joanne   Somert f' the ladies.

Dave   I think he fancies 'imself as a bit of a Lothario.

Joanne   I think he fancies 'imself, yer mean.

Dave   Those sheets could do with a clean.

Joanne   Could they?

Dave   No, I mean . . .

Pause.

The whole flat, I mean. I was thinkin' of payin' a cleaner.

Joanne   Oh, right.

Dave   Once a month or somert. Nowt fancy, just . . . — yer know?

Joanne   'Alf expected some crack 'ouse.

Dave   What?

Joanne   You n' a bunch of refugees. Iraqi freedom fighters or somert.

Dave   Well, it's hardly the Savoy.

Joanne   Shacked up wi' some Pole.

Dave   Who?

Joanne   You n' all the other immigrants. Scrappin' over fake passports.

Dave   Yeah, that's funny.

Joanne   Coked up t' the eye balls.

Dave   Chance'd be a fine thing.

Joanne   Is that a strip club next door?

Dave   It is, yeah.

Joanne   Classy.

Dave   Can I make you somethin' to eat?

Joanne *continues looking at the bits and pieces on the bedside cabinet.*

Long pause.

Dave   Thought yer might be hungry, Joanne, all that travellin'.

Long pause.

All that way, I mean.

Joanne *finds and removes a* Marie Claire *magazine.*

Long pause.

Dave   Joanne . . . —

Joanne   Where is she then?

Dave   Who?

Joanne   *Marie Claire.*

Pause.

Marie Claire, look.

Dave   Oh . . . –

Joanne *flicks through the copy of* Marie Claire.

Dave   Oh, that.

Joanne   Yer readin' this?

Dave   No, not . . . –

Joanne   Can't quite see it meself.

Dave   Not really.

Joanne   Even if it has got Angelina on the front.

Dave   Not if I can help it, no.

Joanne *flicks through the magazine.*

Long pause.

Give me somert t' read when I get back tonight. Slimmin' tips.

Dave   'Elp yerself, yeah.

Joanne   I've lost half a stone since Christmas.

Dave   'Ave yer?

Joanne   Been a right fatty-fat-fat me. Yer sure she won't mind?

Dave   I expect she'll manage.

Joanne   Does she even know I'm 'ere?

Pause.

I'm not bothered.

Dave   No, she's . . .

Joanne   Out the way.

Dave   Sorry?

Joanne   Yer've sent 'er on 'er merry way.

Dave   I don't follow.

Pause.

No, she's out with friends. She's . . . —

Joanne   She's not goin' t' come burstin' through that door?

Dave   It doesn't work like that.

Joanne   'Ow does it work?

Pause.

Dave   It's nothin' . . . —

Joanne   It's temporary.

Dave   Yeah.

Pause.

Yeah, it's one of the few buildings weren't hit by the Blitz.

Joanne   Oh, that's lucky.

Dave   Yer can see all the original fixtures n' fittings if yer look. Yer can see where they've partitioned it into flats.

Joanne   I expect this used to be one big bathroom or somert.

Dave   Yer can judge it by the stairwell, yeah. They've even built offices down in the basement.

Joanne   Pretty popular then, yeah?

Dave   Oh, yeah, there's about thirty-odd bars in this area alone.

Joanne   Really?

Dave   It's like fuckin' *Blade Runner* or somert at the weekend. What with the licensing hours.

Joanne   Keeping you up all night are they?

Dave   They're really trendy.

Joanne   Are they?

Dave   Photographers, artists. Yer get a lot of bands playing. Lot of students, I think.

Joanne   Right.

Dave   That and all yer City kids seein' in the weekend.

Joanne   Like you, yer mean.

Dave   The neighbours.

Joanne   Who?

Dave   The new neighbours, they've just moved in downstairs. Derek and Yan.

Joanne   Derek and who?

Dave   Yan. She's Chinese. They're on the first floor downstairs, they're very friendly.

Joanne   They sound it.

Dave   No, I helped 'em move their stuff in the other weekend. They're very young, I mean.

Joanne   That's good then.

Dave   Them and the arsehole upstairs.

Joanne   Who?

Dave   The arsehole lives above us.

Joanne   Oh, right.

Dave   Danny.

Joanne   And he's an arsehole is he?

Dave   He's like Bob the bloody Builder or somert. Pullin' up his floorboards at two in the morning.

Joanne   Must be annoying.

Dave   Playing his music at full blast. Depeche Mode.

Joanne   I wunt stand for it me.

Dave   He's only twenty-three or somert. Yer'd think he owned the fuckin' building. Him n' the thousand bastard construction firms rippin' up the neighbourhood f' the last twelve months n' all. Scaffoldin' towers left, right n' centre. Pneumatic drills at half past eight in the mornin'. It's like havin' knives driven into yer skull.

Joanne   Best get movin' then 'ant yer?

Dave   I intend to, yeah.

Long pause.

Once I'm . . .

Pause.

Yer know?

Joanne   You n' yer girlfriend.

Dave   She's not my girlfriend.

Joanne   Could just say yer binned it then cunt yer?

Dave   What?

Joanne   Say yer bagged it up for recyclin' or somert. Doin' yer bit f 'the environment.

Dave   I don't think she's that type.

Joanne   What type?

Dave   The recyclin' type.

Joanne   Int she?

Dave   No. I don't think . . . –

Joanne   What type is she then?

Dave   It's not something we really talk about.

Joanne   Dunt she care about 'er carbon footprint?

Dave   Her what?

Joanne   Dunt she give much thought to her emissions?

Dave   Yer takin' the piss.

Joanne   I thought that's what people like you did.

Dave   People like who?

Joanne   'Ow old is she then?

Dave   What?

Joanne   All legal is it?

Dave   Don't be stupid . . .

Joanne   All legal and above board? – Don't worry, I've not come t' pass judgement.

Dave   Yer don't 'ave t' pass judgement, Joanne.

Long pause.

'Ere.

Joanne   What?

Dave   No. I'll . . .

Long pause.

Joanne   What?

Dave   No, that bus.

Pause.

That bus, yer know? The 26. The one they tried to bomb.

Joanne   What about it?

Dave   That were just round the corner from 'ere.

Joanne   Was it?

Dave   Literally. Just round the corner by the church. Yer'll see it when yer next go out.

Joanne   Oh.

Dave   Come back from work and there's fuckin' meat wagons everywhere.

Joanne   Fancy.

Dave   Everywhere's taped off. All the streets, the shops, the whole fuckin' parade round the back. One week after July the seventh, and there's me.

Joanne   There's you, Dave.

Dave   I mean it's worlds apart from owt . . .

Pause.

Joanne   From owt you've ever . . . ?

Dave   I mean, we're only five minutes walk from Bethnal Green. The mosque like, the community.

Joanne   Did yer see any bodies?

Dave   Sorry?

Joanne   Dead bodies. Did yer see any?

Pause.

Dave   What?

Joanne   Don't tell me yer dint look.

Dave   I don't think anyone were killed that day were they?

Joanne   Weren't they?

Dave   No. They weren't.

Joanne   Not much of a story then is it?

Pause.

Dave   I'm just sayin' aren't I? It's somethin' that happened.

Joanne   I'm impressed.

Dave   It's somethin' that happened to me.

Pause.

It's good t' see yer, I mean. I'm glad yer could make it.

Joanne *takes her shoes off.*

Long pause.

Dave   Yeah. Well I'll just . . .

Joanne   Yer know yer grandad's died.

Dave   Has he?

Long pause.

Yeah.

Pause.

Yeah, well, that's . . . –

Joanne   Emphysema.

She hands her shoes to **Dave**.

Long pause.

Dave   Okay.

Joanne   Yer'll have to ask yer mother f' the details.

Dave   Thanks.

Joanne   I'm sorry I don't . . .

Pause.

I don't really . . . –

Dave   No, yer alright, that's . . . –

Joanne   I haven't really kept in touch.

Dave   Course.

Joanne   I went t' the funeral. More out o' courtesy than anything else.

Pause.

Make up the numbers n' that.

Dave   Yeah.

Joanne   This is what, three year back?

Dave   'Ow long?

Joanne   Yer should ring 'er sometime. Yer mum, I mean. I've got 'er number in me phone if yer need it.

Dave   No, that's . . .

Joanne   Yer lucky she's not followed me down 'ere 'erself. Ringin' me at work every five minutes. Christ knows how she got my number, she's like somert off MI5 the way she behaves. I've been convinced she's 'ad me phone tapped all week, the bloody signal on it. — You spoke to 'er?

Dave   Not for years.

Joanne   'Ant yer?

Dave   No, I . . .

Pause.

I haven't really . . . —

Joanne   Me neither.

Dave   Not for decades it feels like.

Joanne   Sometimes bump into 'er in town.

Dave   Right.

Joanne   Food 'all at M n' S.

Dave   Okay.

Joanne   Strugglin' with 'er bags down Chapel Walk. Face on it like doom.

Dave   Yeah, that makes sense.

Joanne   Found 'er cryin' on the steps of the Crucible one time.

Dave   Did yer?

Joanne   During the snooker finals. Just after you left.

Dave   Oh.

Joanne   Just after you abandoned us, I mean.

Pause.

Dave   Oh, okay.

Joanne   In fucking floods she was. On 'er way t' the bus stop, on 'er way home.

Dave   Yeah, that's . . .

Joanne   I tried askin' 'er about it.

Dave   Good.

Joanne   I did try, Dave.

Dave   Well, she was probably upset . . . –

Joanne   Tore one of me earrings out, the bitch.

Dave   She what?

Joanne   Went ballistic, Dave, yeah. Kickin' n' screamin'. Every name under the sun and more. Middle o' town like, on a Saturday. Way 'ome from the match wi' our Phillip.

Dave   Oh . . .

Joanne   And there's her. Springin' up on me like a bloody Rottweiler. Mouthin' off like it were me who drove yer away.

Dave   Oh, well . . .

Joanne   Like I'd buried you under the patio or somert, stupid idiot. Denyin' her of fuckin' grandkids and I'm like 'What?'

Dave   Yer know how emotional she gets.

Joanne   Split me earlobe in two n' all.

Dave   Yeah?

Pause.

Yeah, that's . . . –

Joanne   That's somert what 'appened t' me, Dave.

Long pause.

Course, we can laugh about it now.

Pause.

At the funeral, I mean.

Dave Great, yeah.

Joanne We 'ad a right fuckin' scream about it, Dave, don't look at me like that, it's true.

She removes her tights.

Long pause.

You alright?

Long pause.

Dave . . .

Dave Why shunt I fucking be?

Joanne Yer don't look it.

Dave Why shouldn't I be alright?

Pause.

Joanne Dave . . . –

Dave I'm 'ere aren't I?

Joanne I don't know what you fuckin' are.

Dave Alright, just . . . –

Joanne Yer like some fuckin' shadow or somethin'.

Dave Okay.

Pause.

Okay, yeah . . .

Joanne No offence.

Dave No, that's fair.

Joanne Yer like some ghost, Dave.

Dave   We should probably eat somethin' then shouldn't we?

Joanne   We should what?

Dave   Let me cook yer somethin' at least.

Joanne   I 'ad a sandwich on the train.

Dave   Chorizo salad.

Joanne   What?

Dave   Chorizo and cannellini-bean salad.

Joanne   Are you takin' the piss?

Dave   No, it was in the *Guardian* last weekend.

Joanne   Since when did you read the *Guardian*?

Dave   No, I thought I might . . .

Joanne   Sorry, I shouldn't laugh.

Dave   Eh?

Joanne   Sorry, no, it's just . . .

Long pause.

Sorry.

Dave   Yeah, well. Maybe it's not . . .

Joanne   You haven't changed.

Dave   Haven't I?

Joanne   Ten places at once. Have I come at a bad time?

Dave   Sorry?

Joanne   Shall I come back tomorrow?

She begins removing her earrings and other jewellery.

Pause.

I'm not 'ere t' fight with yer, Dave.

Dave   Sorry, I'm . . .

Joanne   Maybe I should just come back in the morning, eh?

Dave   No, I thought we'd take a walk.

Joanne   What?

Dave   I thought we'd take a walk down the South Bank tomorrow. By the river, I mean. The South Bank.

Joanne   My train leaves at ten.

Dave   Does it?

Joanne   Twenty past ten, Dave, yeah. Gets me back in just after lunch.

Dave   Oh, okay.

Joanne   I've got me IT class at three. What's down the South Bank?

Dave   No, nothing . . .

Pause.

Nothing, I just thought . . . –

Joanne   I mean I can always cancel.

Dave   It really doesn't matter.

Joanne   What's down there like?

Pause.

I'm interested, Dave . . . –

Dave   There's the market. Borough Market.

Joanne   Okay, fine.

Dave   The food there's fantastic.

Joanne   Is it?

Dave   Thought we could go on the Eye. The big wheel, yer must've seen it.

Joanne   I must've, yeah.

Dave   Amazing views.

Joanne   Yeah?

Dave   Yer can walk it from 'ere. Through the City.

Joanne   Great.

Dave   Stop by St Paul's. Over the Millennium Bridge. Tate Modern. Have a look down the Turbine Hall. Shakespeare's Globe.

Joanne   Whatever yer say, Dave.

Dave   Thought it might be nice, that's all. The two of us.

Joanne   'Ant you got work tomorrow?

Dave   What?

Joanne   Don't you work on a Friday?

Dave   Yeah, but . . . –

Joanne   Are yer sure they'll be alright with that?

Dave   That's not the point though is it?

Joanne   What is the point?

Dave   Nothin', I just thought . . .

Pause.

I just fuckin' thought.

Joanne   That's right, cos we don't go on walks back 'ome do we?

Dave   What?

Joanne   We're still livin' in caves, Dave, yeah.

Dave   They do a Jack the Ripper tour.

Joanne   They do what?

Dave   Up the road, up in Whitechapel. There's a Jack the Ripper tour.

Pause.

Joanne   I think I'll get that train if it's all the same.

Dave   I mean, there's Jamie Oliver's restaurant not five minutes . . .

Joanne   Goodge Street.

Dave   What?

Joanne   My hotel. It's over in Goodge Street. That's the Central Line int it?

Dave   Northern.

Joanne   Is it?

Dave   Goodge Street's on the Northern Line.

Joanne   That's not what the man said.

Dave   Yer change at King's Cross.

Joanne   I'm glad I asked.

Dave   It's not far.

Joanne   Can't I walk it?

Dave   On the tube it's not far.

Pause.

Sorry. That sounded really patronising didn't it?

Joanne   Just a bit.

Dave   I'll order you a taxi if yer want.

Joanne   Yer'll do nothin' of the kind.

Dave   If yer'd prefer, I mean. In a bit.

Joanne   The tube's fine thanks.

Dave   I mean, if it's a question of money . . .

Joanne   It's not.

Dave   I don't mind, Joanne.

Joanne   It's not about the money, Dave, yer know that.

Dave   Sorry, yeah.

Joanne   I'm more than capable of takin' care of meself.

Dave   Yeah, I know . . . –

Joanne   You should know that by now.

Dave   I just said so didn't I?

Joanne   It's not like I 'ant 'ad the fuckin' practice.

Dave   *Question Time*'s on tonight.

Joanne   It's what?

Dave   *Question Time*. They've got Martin Amis on the panel, we could watch it.

Long pause.

He makes to leave.

Yeah, well, I'll just . . . –

Joanne   Yer think yer'll just what?

Dave   I think I'll 'ave somethin' stronger if yer don't mind.

Joanne   A drink?

Dave   A fuckin' bottle.

Joanne   You do that, Dave, yeah.

Dave *re-enters the living area, carrying* **Joanne***'s shoes, tights, etc.*

He dumps them on the futon, then moves to the kitchen area. He searches the cupboards and finds a bottle of brandy and a glass.

He pours himself a shot and drinks it.

Pause.

He pours himself a triple shot and drinks another mouthful.

Pause.

He takes the brandy, moves to the office area and sits at his desk.

Sipping the brandy, he ejects a CD from the laptop.

With a marker pen, he writes something on the CD and places it in its case.

As he all does this, **Joanne** *hesitates, then . . .*

Pause.

She straightens the bed.

Pause.

She moves to the bedroom window and peers out at the buildings opposite.

She spies something or someone, and peers closer — her nose touching the glass.

Pause.

She returns to and sits on the edge of the bed.

She gets undressed.

She is about to remove her underwear, when . . .

Dave *re-enters the bedroom, with his brandy and the CD.*

Joanne   D'yer know there's some kid lookin' in?

Dave   Sorry?

Joanne   There's some kid lookin' in from the flats out there.

Pause.

Dave . . . —

Dave   What, sorry?

Joanne   I mean he can't be much older than ten.

Dave   Oh, him.

Joanne   Peerin' through the curtains in his pyjamas, the dirty bastard.

Dave   Yeah, I know, he's always . . .

Joanne *removes her underwear.*

Pause.

Joanne   He's always what?

Dave   I think he must just be bored or somert.

Joanne   Yer've spoke to 'im?

Dave   I've seen 'im before, I mean.

Joanne   Yer should 'ave a word with 'is parents.

Dave   Well, I don't . . .

Pause.

Hardly breakin' the law though, is 'e?

Joanne   He wants to get 'imsen a girlfriend I reckon.

Dave   Yer don't want to encourage 'im, yer mean.

She reaches for her bag, and for her cigarettes.

She proceeds to light one.

Pause.

Dave *places his brandy and the CD on the bedside cabinet.*

He then moves to the blinds, and pulls them down.

Long pause.

Joanne   Yer don't have to look so nervous, Dave.

Dave   Who said I was nervous?

Joanne   You out o' practice or somert?

Dave   No.

Joanne   Stood there like a bloody hatstand.

Dave   No, yer've had yer hair cut.

Joanne   What?

Pause.

Dave   I said yer've had yer hair cut, Joanne.

Joanne   Yeah, I have.

Dave   That recent?

Joanne   Fairly.

Dave   No, it suits yer.

Joanne   What?

Dave   I like it.

Pause.

Yer hair, I mean.

Joanne   D'yer?

Dave   It's nice.

He sits on the edge of the bed.

The colouring n' . . . n' that, it suits yer.

Joanne   Thanks.

Long pause.

Dave *goes to touch* **Joanne***'s hair.*

Dave   I mean, yer'd never tell . . . —

Joanne (*pushes his hand away*)   Don't.

Dave   Sorry.

Joanne   Just don't alright?

Dave   Sorry, I dint . . . —

Joanne   Try that again and I'll fuckin' flatten yer.

Dave   No, I mean it, it's really . . .

Long pause.

It's really great to see you, Joanne.

Joanne   Don't tell me yer havin' second thoughts.

Dave   Of course not, it's just . . . —

Joanne   I'm ovulatin'.

Dave   Yeah, and that's a good thing isn't it?

Joanne *climbs into bed.*

Long pause.

Dave   Westminster Abbey.

Joanne   What?

Dave   The two of us, I mean.

Joanne   Yer thought the two of us might what?

Dave   I don't know, just . . .

Pause.

Anything.

Joanne   Yer thought we might go sightseein'?

Dave   No, not if yer don't want.

Joanne   Yer thought we might take a trip down memory lane?

Dave   Oh, come on, Joanne . . . –

Joanne   Like I'm supposed t' come fallin' into your arms or somert?

Dave   No, that's not it at all . . . –

Joanne   After all you put me through.

Dave   Don't be stupid.

Joanne   After ten years of fuckin' silence.

Dave   Don't be stupid, Joanne, no.

Long pause.

Of course not.

Pause.

I mean. Not if you don't . . . –

Joanne   There's some lad mags in me bag if yer need it.

Dave   Sorry?

Joanne   Only if yer need it mind.

She picks up the copy of Marie Claire, *and flicks through it.*

Long pause.

That is unless . . . –

Dave   No, I'm fine.

Joanne   They don't really go topless in *Marie Claire* d'they? Angelina Jolie, I mean. I don't suppose she'd ever . . . –

Dave   She doesn't, no, yer right.

Joanne   Pity.

Dave   Yeah.

Joanne   Most beautiful woman in the world.

Dave   T' some maybe.

Joanne   Big flappin' lips. CGI tits.

Over the following, the muffled – but audible – noise of drilling and hammering begins to be heard from the flat above.

Joanne *pulls out a couple of lad mags from her handbag.*

She flicks through them.

Long pause.

Dave   Joanne . . . –

Joanne   There's a feature on Abi Titmuss in this one.

Dave   What?

Joanne   Abi Titmuss, look.

She flicks open the magazine for **Dave** *and offers it to him.*

Pause.

Joanne   Aren't yer interested at least?

Dave   That's Abi Titmuss is it?

Joanne   She's got her tits out, Dave, yeah.

Dave   Oh.

Long pause.

Great, yeah . . . –

Joanne   Lucy Pinder. Sarah Harding.

Dave   Who?

Joanne   Girls Aloud. The blonde one.

Dave   Somethin' for everyone, yeah?

Pause.

Okay.

He takes the other magazines.

Okay, great . . . –

Joanne   I mean it's only if it helps.

Dave   It does help.

Joanne   Does it?

Dave   Yeah.

Pause.

Yeah, it's really helpful, Joanne.

Joanne   Course yer can always pay me back my train fare.

Dave   Yeah, I know.

Joanne   I mean if yer'd rather not . . . –

Dave   I've just said so 'ant I?

Joanne   I'd rather yer were honest with me, that's all.

Dave   I am being fuckin' honest.

Joanne   Yer know I'm goin' t' turn forty next month.

Dave   Yeah, I know that.

Joanne   Well then.

Dave   Jesus Christ, Joanne, I'm 'ere aren't I?

Joanne   Ten years of cleanin' up after your mess.

Dave   Alright, I know, it were me who wrote to you, remember?

Joanne   Oh, I remember alright.

Dave   Joanne, please . . . –

Joanne   Beggin' for every penny I can lay my hands on, while you vanish into thin fuckin' air.

Dave   That weren't it at all . . . –

Joanne   Weren't it?

Dave   You know that, Joanne.

Joanne   Forty year old wi' nowt but me fuckin' Freeview for company? I'd say that were pretty bang on.

Dave   I never abandoned anyone.

Joanne   Try tellin' that t' yer mother.

Dave   You leave her out o' this.

Joanne   We thought yer'd been killed f' fucksake!

Long pause.

Dave   I mean . . . –

Joanne   What's the tube of Canesten for?

Dave   Eh?

Joanne   'Ave you got thrush?

Dave   Don't be stupid.

Joanne   Chlamydia then?

Dave   No, I . . .

Pause.

I haven't, no.

Joanne   Good.

Long pause.

That's good then, Dave.

Dave   Yeah.

Joanne   I'm not goin' t' hang about for ever.

Dave   No one's said that.

Joanne   We had an agreement dint we?

Long pause.

Dave . . . –

Dave (*as he leaves*)   Just give me a minute would yer?

He exits the bedroom, with the magazines, and enters the bathroom, slamming the door behind him.

He switches on the bathroom light.

He moves to the toilet, and places the magazines on the floor and the wine glass on the side of the bath.

While he does this, **Joanne** *finishes her cigarette and stubs it out.*

She makes to take the wine bottle, for which she has to climb out of bed to grab it from the chest of drawers, opposite the bed.

She takes the bottle of wine from off the chest of drawers.

Sitting on the edge of the bed, she takes her glass and refills it.

She then places the bottle back.

She sips from the wine glass.

Pause.

She catches sight of her reflection in the mirror.

Pause.

She pulls the covers up around her, disguising her body.

The drilling and hammering cause the lights in the flat to flicker momentarily.

Pause.

She looks back to her reflection, and messes with her hair.

She turns away from the mirror, and drinks from the wine glass.

The lights flicker momentarily.

Long pause.

She gathers the covers around her body, and climbs over the bed.

She moves to the full-length mirror and turns it round so that she can no longer see her reflection.

Pause.

She retrieves the bottle and the wine glass and refills it.

She drinks.

Long pause.

Pulling the covers around herself, she stands and heads to the window.

She peers through the blinds.

The lights flicker.

Long pause.

She opens the blinds a touch and looks through the window at the opposite flats.

As she does all this, **Dave** *unbuckles his belt, and removes his trousers and pants.*

He sits on the toilet seat.

He sips from his wine glass, then puts it back on the side of the bath.

He picks up the magazine and opens it up on the bookmarked page.

He plays with himself as he looks at the pictures.

The lights flicker.

Long pause.

He changes his mind, flicks through the magazine and finds another page.

He places the magazine on the floor, by his feet, folding the pages out, and using one of his feet as a paperweight.

Looking at the magazine, he takes another sip from his wine, and then proceeds to play with himself.

Long pause.

He grabs the towel that is hanging on the bathroom radiator.

He stands, then wraps and ties the towel around his waist.

He gathers his trousers and pants from the floor and holds them under one arm.

He exits the bathroom, and re-enters the bedroom.

Joanne *is looking through the window, oblivious to his return.*

Dave *places his clothes by the side of the bed, then exits the bedroom.*

He moves to and re-enters the bathroom.

He takes the magazine and the glass of wine.

He exits the bathroom, switching the light off as he goes.

He re-enters the bedroom, places the magazine on top of the letters on the bedside cabinet, and sits on the edge of the bed, holding his glass of wine.

The drilling and hammering continue, causing the lights to flicker.

Long pause.

Joanne *pulls the blinds down and sits on the opposite end of the bed.*

She finds another cigarette from the packet and lights it.

Long pause.

Joanne   It's nice.

Dave   Sorry?

Joanne   The wine. It's very nice.

Dave   I think I'll stick t' the brandy if it's all the same.

Joanne   Got a fuckin' kick on it at least.

Dave   Yeah, thanks.

Long pause.

Yeah, it had a decent write-up.

Joanne   Did it?

Dave   Four stars.

Joanne   Oh . . .

Dave   In the . . . paper n' that. In the supplement.

Joanne   Oh, right.

Long pause.

Dave   And that's rare for Sainsbury's.

Joanne   I'll drink anything me.

Dave   I mean it's as good as owt yer'll find in Waitrose.

Joanne   Is it?

Long pause.

Dave   Yeah, it's . . . —

Joanne   Aren't yer goin' t' get in?

Pause.

Aren't yer goin' t' get it in with me, Dave?

Long pause.

D'yer need me to do anything for yer?

Dave No. I'm . . .

Pause.

Really, I'm . . .

Joanne Yer look like yer head's goin' to burst open.

Dave Does it?

Joanne Yer look like yer goin' t' combust, Dave, yeah. Does he always make that noise?

Dave Yer'll get used to it.

Joanne 'Ow old is 'e? Twenty-eight?

Dave Twenty-three.

Joanne Shunt he be out livin' it up or somert?

Dave Would yer like me to ask 'im for yer?

Joanne He's hardly settin' the mood.

Dave I'll ask 'im t' join us then shall I?

Joanne I'm only sayin' . . . –

Dave What d'yer want, the man from fuckin' Milk Tray?

Joanne If it makes it any easier . . . –

Dave How can it be any easier? Jesus Christ . . . –

Joanne I'm jokin' with yer, yer dimwit.

Dave D'yer see me fuckin' laughin'? Sat 'ere with me cock out.

Joanne Oh, come on, Dave, it's not like we've never done it before.

Dave Yeah, and I don't need you . . . –

Joanne It's not like we're fuckin' strangers.

Dave Yeah, I know that.

Joanne   We aborted three of 'em, remember?

Long pause.

Dave   Alright.

Pause.

Alright, just . . .

Joanne   I might need some warmin' up.

Dave   What?

Joanne   Yer might have t' warm me up.

Long pause.

Sorry.

Dave   No.

Pause.

No, that's . . .

Joanne   This isn't easy f'me either, yer know?

Long pause.

Please.

Long pause.

Dave . . . –

Dave   No, I know that.

Joanne   Wet yer fingers.

Dave   Eh?

Joanne   Wet yer fingers and yer thumb.

She stubs her cigarette out.

Long pause.

Well, go on.

Pause.

Go on, Dave.

Dave I'm doin' it aren't I?

He switches the bedside lamp off.

Darkness.

He removes the towel and climbs into bed with **Joanne**, *pulling the covers over himself.*

Long pause.

The sound of the hammering and drilling continues in short, muffled bursts.

Joanne Dave . . . –

Dave Just a minute I said.

Joanne But . . . –

Dave Give me a minute.

Long pause.

Joanne Can't yer find it?

Long pause.

Can't yer find it?

Pause.

Just . . . there.

Pause.

Just there. That's it, right there.

Pause.

Where yer were before.

Pause.

Where yer were, go on. It's not a punchbag.

Very, very long pause.

Don't do that, Dave –

Dave *climbs out from under the sheets.*

Joanne   Dave, please . . . –

Dave   I can't think straight.

Joanne   You just had it, go on.

Dave   I can't fuckin' think straight, Joanne.

He switches the bedside lamp on.

He climbs off **Joanne**, *and sits on the edge of the bed.*

He pulls the towel back over his waist and legs.

Long pause.

Joanne *takes her drink from the bedside cabinet and sips it.*

Dave *doesn't move from the edge of the bed.*

Long pause.

Joanne   Here.

Dave   What?

Joanne   Here.

She hands **Dave** *her drink.*

Joanne   Quiet as mice, go on.

She kneels up on the bed, behind **Dave** *and strokes his shoulders and chest.*

Long pause.

Joanne   That okay f'yer?

Long pause.

She strokes **Dave**'s *body, then slips her hand under the towel.*

Long pause.

Joanne   Dave.

*She has her hand under the towel, between **Dave**'s legs.*

Long pause.

Joanne   Tell me if I'm . . . –

Pause.

Tell me if I'm pullin' it too 'ard.

Pause.

If yer want me t' pull the skin back.

Pause.

If yer want me squeeze the tip.

Dave   The wireless is switched on.

Long pause.

Joanne   Dave.

Long pause.

Is there somethin' the . . . ?

Dave   The fuckin' wireless is switched on.

*He pulls **Joanne**'s hand out from under the towel.*

Joanne   But . . . –

Dave   The wireless, Joanne, just stop it will yer?!

Pause.

Joanne   Are you alright?

Dave   I've left it hooked up t' the computer –

Joanne   Yer've left what?

Dave   Don't you laugh at me.

Joanne   I'm not laughing.

Dave   Don't you dare laugh at me, Joanne, I mean it!

He slams the wine glass on the cabinet, then grabs his clothes off the floor and, over the following, frantically gets dressed.

Pause.

Laugh in my fuckin' face. D'yer know what that's meant t' do t' yer?!

Joanne   Alright, I won't.

Dave   D'yer know what that does t' yer brain cells, Joanne?! F' Christ's sake . . . —

He exits the bedroom, carrying the rest of his clothes, and enters the living space.

The noise of the drilling is getting louder.

He moves to the futon, sits.

(*As he sits.*)   — . . . you've only just walked in through the fuckin' door!

He pulls on and buttons up the rest of his clothes.

Stupid fuckin' . . . —

*Following this, **Dave** moves to the office area, and wrestles with the cables in an attempt to unplug the wireless and shut down his computer.*

*Through all this, **Joanne** wraps the sheets around herself, and exits the bedroom.*

*She stands by the bedroom doorway, watching **Dave**.*

Joanne   Is there somethin' yer want t' talk about?

Dave *continues.*

Pause.

Joanne   Dave . . . —

Dave   I'm doin' it aren't I?

Joanne   I mean, it's nothin' . . . —

Dave   Just leave it, Joanne!

Joanne   It's nothin' to be ashamed of . . . —

Dave   I can't think!

Joanne   Alright . . . —

Dave   I can't think with all 'is fuckin' noise! Gi' over fuckin' followin' me will yer?!

He throws the cables back down, and makes for the front door.

Pause.

Joanne   Dave . . . —

Dave (*as he exits*)   This is my fuckin' flat, stay where you are!

He exits through the front door, slamming the door behind him.

The drilling and hammering continues.

Long pause.

Joanne *re-enters the bedroom, and sits on the edge of the bed.*

She takes her glass of wine and sips from it.

Pause.

She puts the wine glass down.

She picks up her underwear and puts it back on.

Pause.

She goes to pick up the rest of her clothes from the floor, when . . .

Pause.

She spots the tracksuit bottoms and T-shirt that **Dave** *hid under the bed.*

She pulls them out.

She looks at them. The T-shirt has a printed logo on the front: 'The Libertines' or 'Arctic Monkeys', or a similar rock band.

Pause.

She puts the T-shirt and the tracksuit bottoms on.

The drilling and hammering upstairs suddenly stops.

Long pause.

She moves before the mirror.

She looks at her reflection, dressed in the new outfit.

Pause.

She strikes a pose.

Pause.

She messes up her hair.

She strikes a pose.

Pause.

She returns to the edge of the bed and sits down.

She takes a cigarette from her packet, puts it in her mouth (in the style of Keith Richards), and lights it.

Pause.

She hesitates.

Pause.

She moves to the bedroom window.

She pulls the blinds up, and peers out to the opposite flats.

Pause.

She taps on the window with her knuckles.

Pause.

Standing before the window she takes off the 'Libertines' T-shirt.

Pause.

She removes her bra.

Pause.

She peers out of the window.

Pause.

She taps on the window with her knuckles, when . . .

Dave *re-enters through the front door, shutting the door behind him.*

He stands by the doorway and buttons up his shirt.

Joanne *pulls the blinds down.*

Pause.

Joanne *returns to the edge of the bed, and stubs out her cigarette.*

She puts on the T-shirt.

As she does this, and over the next, **Dave** *straightens his shirt and moves to the office area.*

He sits at his desk.

He removes his mobile phone from his pocket, turns it on and checks/scrolls through a couple of new text messages.

The following dialogue takes place between the two rooms.

Joanne (*from the bedroom*)   Feelin' better now are yer?

Long pause.

Dave.

Dave (*from the living area*)   What, sorry?

Joanne (*from the bedroom*)   Everythin' alright?

Dave (*from the living area*)   I think we'll be alright for a bit, yeah.

Pause.

Before the evening's out at least.

Joanne (*from the bedroom*)   Punch his lights out did yer?

Dave (*from the living area*)   No, it's his bathroom.

Joanne (*from the bedroom*)   It's his what?

Dave (*from the living area*)   He's doin' up his bathroom.

Joanne (*from the bedroom*)   Oh, right.

Dave (*from the living area*)   Yeah.

Pause.

Yeah, it's lookin' pretty good. Mirrors on both walls.

Joanne (*from the bedroom*)   That's good then int it?

Dave (*from the living area*)   Power shower. Remote sensor . . .

Pause.

Remote sensor thingamajig.

Joanne (*from the bedroom*)   Don't tell me yer jealous.

Dave (*from the living area*)   Fuck off, jealous. What, of him?

Joanne (*from the bedroom*)   I'm only sayin'.

Dave (*from the living area*)   That little nondescript? – Yeah, well don't.

Joanne (*from the bedroom*)   If you're going to get stroppy about it . . . –

Dave (*from the living area*)   Arrogant bastard.

Joanne (*from the bedroom*)   What did you call me?

Dave (*from the living area*)   I said he's an arrogant little bastard.

Long pause.

Dave *finishes reading his text messages and tosses the mobile phone on the desk.*

He hesitates, while . . .

Joanne *sparks another cigarette, placing the pack in the tracksuit-bottom pocket.*

She stands and picks up the two wine glasses.

Dave *moves to, and enters, the bathroom, shutting the door behind him.*

Joanne *exits the bedroom, and enters the living area.*

She goes to the kitchen area, and places the wine glasses on the counter.

She finds the wine bottle.

She proceeds to pour two fresh glasses of wine.

As she does this, **Dave** *moves to the toilet, and lifts up the lid.*

He has a piss.

Pause.

He accidentally pisses on the floor.

Pause.

He flushes the toilet, and grabs a length of toilet roll.

He squats down on the floor, and wipes the piss up off the floor and from around the basin/rim.

He throws the toilet paper into the toilet.

Pause.

He moves to the sink, and washes his hands.

While he does this, **Joanne** *has filled up the wine glasses.*

She rummages through the cupboards, and removes the ingredients for the chorizo and cannellini-bean salad.

She places these on the side.

Meanwhile, **Dave** *turns off the taps and is about to exit the bathroom.*

Pause.

He hesitates.

Pause.

He returns to the toilet, shuts the lid and sits down.

Pause.

He hesitates.

Pause.

He rummages through his pockets.

As he does this, the mobile phone that he abandoned on the desk begins to vibrate.

Joanne *sees/hears the phone vibrating.*

She hesitates.

Pause.

She leaves the kitchen area, and moves to the desk.

She is about to pick up the phone, but it stops ringing.

Pause.

Dave *stops rummaging through his pockets.*

Pause.

He hesitates, while . . .

Joanne *picks up the phone and returns to the kitchen area, placing it on the counter.*

She unwraps the chorizo sausage from its packaging, while . . .

Dave *stands and, quickly checking his reflection in the mirror, exits the bathroom, shutting the door behind him.*

He moves through the living space, and enters the bedroom.

Pause.

He sits on the bed, and looks for his socks and shoes.

He finds them and puts them on.

As he does this, **Joanne** *finds a knife and begins to chop the chorizo sausage.*

Pause.

The mobile phone vibrates.

Joanne *picks up the phone, presses a button and puts it to her ear.*

Long pause.

Dave *has put on his socks and shoes.*

He stands and goes to the bedside cabinet.

He picks up the CD.

He opens the lid, closes the lid.

Pause.

He looks for his glass of wine, but cannot find it.

As **Joanne** *finishes listening to the voice message and presses a button to end the call . . .*

Dave *re-enters the living space, with the CD.*

He hesitates.

Joanne *puts the phone back on the kitchen counter.*

She hesitates.

Long pause.

Dave *moves to the kitchen area, and takes his glass of wine.*

Pause.

He moves to the office area and sits by the desk.

He places the CD on the desk, and sips his wine.

Pause.

Joanne *takes the kitchen knife and begins chopping up the chorizo sausage.*

Dave *peers through the blinds.*

Pause.

He watches **Joanne**.

Pause.

He picks up the CD.

Long pause.

Dave   I burnt yer a CD.

Joanne   Did yer?

Dave   Yeah, I . . .

Pause.

Burnt yer a few tunes yer might like.

Joanne   Oh . . . –

Dave   Somethin' t' take back with yer, I mean. Somethin' f' when yer get home.

Joanne   Oh, that's nice.

Dave   Yeah, I mean that's . . .

Pause.

That's what I thought.

Joanne   Has it got any Beatles on it?

Dave   One or two.

Joanne   I am surprised.

Dave   No, I was thinkin' of you, I mean.

Joanne   I see.

Dave   There's a track-listin' on the box. I think yer'll like it.

Joanne   No, I'm sure . . . –

Dave   Just, yer know?

Joanne   Thanks, that's . . .

Dave   Some songs yer might not 'ave got.

Long pause.

I can play it through the plasma screen, through the speakers. Yer'd be astonished at the quality.

Long pause.

I can stick the fuckin' thing on now, Joanne.

Joanne *snatches the CD off* **Dave***.*

She inspects the track list.

Pause.

Joanne   This your idea of foreplay?

Dave   No.

Joanne   Well I should hope not n' all.

She reads the tracklist on the CD.

Pause.

Dave   No. I just thought . . . –

Joanne   Elvis Costello, Sam Cooke.

Dave   Yeah.

Pause.

Yeah, it's . . . –

Joanne   Not many women on this is there?

Dave   There's Joni Mitchell.

Joanne *puts the CD down and continues chopping the chorizo.*

Long pause.

Dave   I made it for you, Joanne.

Long pause.

Joanne . . . –

Joanne   Yeah. I heard yer the first time.

Dave   It belongs to me.

Joanne   Alright . . . –

Dave   No. the plasma screen, it's mine.

Pause.

That and the laptop, the whole . . .

Pause.

. . . the whole set-up, I mean. The wardrobe through there, the blinds. The fuckin' pictures on the walls.

Joanne   They're all yours are they?

Dave   The crockery, Joanne, yeah. – Don't think I 'ant got plans.

Joanne   I don't.

Dave   Don't think I can't see the bigger picture.

Joanne   Did I say that?

Dave   Yer don't 'ave t' say a thing. Joanne, no, I'll take yer shoppin' if yer want.

Joanne   What?

Dave   I'll take yer down Knightsbridge. Harrods, I mean.

Pause.

Yeah. I will.

Pause.

I'll treat yer, Joanne, yer'd like that.

Long pause.

Yer'd like that, Joanne, I know yer would.

Joanne   I'd like yer to gi' over fuckin' whinin'.

Dave   D'yer know how hard I work at my job?

Joanne   No, you tell me.

Dave   Have you any idea of the hours I put in?

Joanne   Tell me all about it, Dave, go on.

Dave   I could buy you a fuckin' diamond with what I earn.

Joanne   Can I have that in writin'?

Dave   Name the price.

Joanne   What?

Dave   Name the price.

She chops the chorizo.

Long pause.

Joanne   Should've just said if yer weren't up to it.

Dave   I am up to it.

Joanne   Waste my time.

Dave   I'm fuckin' up to it, Joanne, alright?

Joanne   Go back on yer promise.

Dave   I told yer I can't think with that noise.

Joanne   What, did it just slip yer mind to fuckin' tell me?

Dave   It's a studio flat.

Joanne   It's what?

Dave   It's a studio flat, for Christ's sake, yer get what you pay for. I can't stop other people . . .

Joanne *continues chopping the chorizo.*

Long pause.

Dave   Sleep on 'ere.

Joanne   What?

Dave   No, I mean, I can. I can do that. I mean.

Pause.

I can sleep on the futon tonight, I don't mind.

Joanne   Oh . . . –

Dave   No, I'd like that.

Joanne   Would yer?

Dave   I'd be more than happy, Joanne.

Joanne   Right.

Dave   Yer've always hated hotels anyway.

Joanne *chops the chorizo.*

Long pause.

Dave   Remember?

Long pause.

Remember, Joanne?

Long pause.

Jesus Christ, put it down will yer?

She continues.

Long pause.

I don't want yer doin' that.

Joanne   Yer look like yer goin' t' pass out.

Dave   Put it down I said.

Joanne   Yer look like yer could do wi' it, Dave, yer've gone pale.

Dave   Put the knife down, will yer?

Pause.

Yer not even using it right.

Joanne   Yeah, well, you were the one . . . —

Dave   D'yer know how much that cost me?

Joanne   You're the one insistin' we stuff our fuckin' faces.

Dave   That's Sabatier, yer dimwit!

She continues.

Long pause.

I'm warnin' you, Joanne.

Pause.

I'm more than capable of cooking my own fuckin' supper.

Long pause.

Look, give it over, come on.

Joanne   Don't you touch me.

Dave   The fuckin' knife, I said, yer going to wreck it.

Long pause.

The fucking knife . . . —

He wrestles the knife out of her hand, and pushes her aside.

. . . Joanne, hand it over!

Joanne   Ow! Don't you fuckin' . . . —

Dave   Give it back to me, sit down!

Joanne   Grab at me, Dave, I'll . . . —

Dave   Sit down! . . . —

Over the next, **Dave** *grabs* **Joanne** *and drags her out of the kitchen area and into the living space, throwing her down onto the futon.*

Dave   Sit the fuck down, get down!

Joanne (*fighting back*)   Yer mad fuckin' bastard . . . —

Dave (*dragging her*)   Get away from me, you 'ear?

Joanne (*fighting back*)   Don't you ever touch me like . . . —

Dave *shoves* **Joanne** *onto the futon.*

Dave   Sit down and shut up!

Joanne   Grab at me, yer fuckin' maniac!

Dave   Yeah, and yer can take that fuckin' T-shirt off n' all.

Joanne   I can take what off? Don't you come near me —

Dave   Take it off, it's not yours!

Joanne   Don't touch me, don't . . . —

Dave   Take it off I said . . . —

He grabs **Joanne** *and tries pulling the tracksuit bottoms and top off her.*

Joanne *fights back, punching, kicking and scratching him.*

Dave   . . . Take it off! I'll rip yer fuckin' head off. Joanne, come on!

Joanne   Jesus Christ . . . –

Dave   It dunt fuckin' belong to you!

Joanne   Hands off me, hands . . . –

She boots and scratches **Dave** *away.*

Joanne   . . . off!

Dave   It dunt belong to you, they're not yours!

Joanne   You try that one more fuckin' time.

Dave   Yer'll do as I fuckin' well . . . –

He grabs the knife from the side.

. . . tell yer, Joanne, you 'ear?!

Long pause.

Joanne . . . –

Joanne   D'yer want me to call the police?

Dave   It's gone, look, it's gone.

He puts the knife down on the counter.

Long pause.

I've put it down, Joanne, see?

Long pause.

Joanne.

He slowly moves towards her.

Long pause.

Joanne, please . . . –

Joanne   Yer bleedin', look.

Dave   What?

Joanne   There's blood runnin' down your face.

Dave *touches his face.*

There are scratch marks on his forehead and cheeks that are bleeding. He sees the blood on his fingers.

Long pause.

Dave   Oh . . .

Pause.

Oh. Yeah, that's . . .

Joanne   That's blood, Dave, yeah. Will she be alright with that?

Dave   Will who be alright? – I've told yer before, she's nothin'.

Joanne   How are yer goin' to explain that one at work?

Pause.

Dave . . . –

Dave   I'm not.

Joanne   Won't they be bothered?

Dave   No, I'm not . . . –

Joanne   All the hours yer put in.

Dave   Look . . . –

Joanne   The amount you earn.

Dave   I'm not going to do that, Joanne, fuck off will yer?

Joanne   They won't be bothered then I take it. – Are they not bothered about you?

Dave   Look . . . –

Joanne   Are you that much of a nondescript?

Dave   I don't have to explain myself to anyone.

Joanne   Does anyone even notice that you're there? What d'yer do again?

Dave   I'm not goin' t' let you . . . —

Joanne   What's yer job title again?

Dave   Eh?

Joanne   What d'they call yer? – It's not a trick question, Dave.

Dave   I've told yer before, it's an agency.

Joanne   It's what?

Dave   I work for an agency.

Joanne   What agency?

Dave   A recruitment agency. I'm freelance. – Jesus Christ, what is this?

Joanne   Alright, I'm only askin'.

Dave   What are yer, the Inland Revenue now?

Joanne   I'm only tryin' t' paint a picture . . . —

Dave   Shall I print you off a CV while yer at it?

Joanne   No . . . —

Dave   Fuckin' remittance.

Joanne   What?

Dave   My fuckin' remittance, look! 'Ere!

He grabs a letter from the desk, and throws it at **Joanne**.

Joanne   Yer gettin' hysterical again, Dave.

Dave   Get it fuckin' framed, go on!

Joanne   I think yer'd better . . . –

Dave   Hang it t' the bedroom ceilin' why not!

Joanne   I think yer should calm down don't you?

Dave   I am fuckin' calm!

He moves to the kitchen area and refills his wine glass.

Jesus Christ, Joanne, have you totally lost the fuckin' plot?

Joanne   Beatin' up on women.

Dave   I did what?

Joanne   Pushin' me around.

Dave   Oh, come on, grow up.

Joanne   Is this how you get your kicks or somert?

Dave   I hardly touched yer f' fucksake. I hardly touched yer, don't . . . –

Joanne   Does she know about your problem?

Dave   What problem? If you think . . . –

Joanne   You n' yer limp fuckin' dick.

Dave   Joanne, please . . . –

Joanne   Well, does she?

Pause.

Dave   Look . . . –

Joanne   Does she sit n' nod n' blame herself for your hang-ups? I bet yer bloody let 'er n' all, poor bitch.

Dave   Yer know nothin' about 'er, Joanne, it's different.

Joanne   What?

Dave   It's just different, alright? For Christ's sake . . . –

Joanne   Off 'er face on God knows what.

Dave   It's different when it's someone who knows what they're doin' at least.

Joanne   Excuse me?

Dave   That's right, Joanne, yeah. When it's not some overweight, middle-aged cunt, dressed up like a schoolteacher. When it's a bleached-blonde nineteen-year-old with tits like two meringues. When we've been up all night snortin' charlie and she's suckin' off the end o' my cock. – Yeah, that makes a difference, Joanne, is that alright f'yer is it?

Joanne   'Ave yer told 'er we're still married?

Dave   No.

Joanne   Are you plannin' to?

Dave   No.

Pause.

No, I'm . . . –

Joanne   She doesn't know then I take it?

Dave   Look . . . –

Joanne   She doesn't know about the debts you left me and my family with?

Dave   That's not the . . . –

Joanne   The thousands o' pounds I'm still payin' off.

Dave   That's not the fuckin' point, Joanne!

Pause.

No, of course not, I've told yer, it's . . . –

Joanne   It's nothin', yeah, I gathered that.

Dave   She's insignificant, Joanne, I hardly know her.

Joanne   'Ow come she's screaming down the phone at yer then?

Dave   She's what?

Joanne   Have you had a fallin'-out or somert?

Dave   She said what, sorry?

Joanne   They're on their way to the Academy.

Dave   Where?

Joanne   Brixton Academy. Some Grime Night apparently.

Dave   Some what night?

Joanne   That's right. Dave, they're about to get the tube if yer hurry up. Her and this Denzil bloke whoever he is. Somert about needin' to pay the man off like yer promised.

Dave   Look . . . —

Joanne   Are you supplyin' 'er with drugs, Dave?

Dave   Don't be stupid.

Joanne   D'yer want me to call 'er back?

Dave   Joanne, please . . . —

Joanne   I think yer should do that, Dave, actually. I mean, Christ knows . . . —

Dave   She can take care of herself.

Joanne   She can what?

Dave   She's more than capable, Joanne.

Joanne   Oh, I'm sure she's capable alright.

Dave   No, they're to help her lose weight. The drugs, I mean, the money.

Joanne   They're doing what?

Dave   She's trying to get into the fashion industry. I don't know.

Joanne   No, yer don't know.

Dave   It's a lifestyle, it costs money.

Joanne   What, and you're her manager are yer?

Dave   I hardly know her f' fucksake.

Joanne   Are you her pimp, Dave?

Dave   We met at a nightclub, it was her who came on to me!

Joanne   Yeah, I bet she did.

Dave   Oh, come on, Joanne . . . –

Joanne   Yeah, I bet she saw you comin'. You n' yer plasma screen.

Dave   Are you jealous or somethin'?

Joanne   You n' yer diamond bloody rings, givin' it the great big lovable bear. Some teenager who dunt know any better . . . –

Dave   She's goin' t' turn twenty in October, of course she dunt know any better, she can work that out for herself!

Joanne   Some girl you leave to wander the streets like that.

Dave   Look, if I thought for one minute that she was even remotely . . . –

Joanne   What, yer'd be chargin' out that door?

Dave   Let me finish.

Joanne   Yer'd be racin' over to Brixton in yer Batmobile would yer?

Dave   Yer'd know about it.

Joanne   What?

Dave   Yer'd fuckin' know about it, Joanne.

Joanne   Oh, come off it, yer donkey, yer've only ever been bothered about yerself. They could be wheelin' 'er down A&E for all you fuckin' care. Like you care about any one of us.

Dave   That's not true.

Joanne   You n' yer flash fuckin' flat.

Dave   Alright . . . –

Joanne   You n' yer Gucci fuckin' suit.

Dave   Alright, just . . .

Joanne   Actin' the big man.

Dave   Just settle down . . . –

Joanne   Don't act the big man with me, yer fat fuckin' bastard. I can still see straight through yer.

Dave   But I wasn't . . . –

Joanne   Fuckin' caretaker you.

Dave   I wasn't trying to do anything, Joanne –

Joanne   Yer tenant. – 'Ow old are yer now?

Dave   I'm forty-fuckin'-four.

Joanne   Walled up in this shit'ole.

Dave   This is a prime location for Christ's sake!

Joanne   I know what I see.

Dave   We're in the centre of London, Joanne, look around yer!

Joanne   I know a shit'ole when I see one.

Dave   When you see one!

Joanne   That's right, Dave, yeah, I'm not one of yer little air'eads, I can see with my own two eyes . . . –

Dave   Oh, face it, Joanne, you 'ant got the class.

Joanne   I 'ant got the what?

Dave   You 'ant got the class, yer block'ead. – What did you expect? The Houses of bloody Parliament?

Joanne   Don't you talk down to me like that.

Dave   Get yer facts straight then, retard, this is the centre of London, we're only five minutes from the Bank of England out there.

Joanne   At least I still know where I come from.

Dave   Oh, fuck off, 'come from'. Yer'll be pullin' out yer flat cap next!

Joanne   Yer don't even know who you are any more.

Dave   And I suppose yer'd rather it were somert off Brookside bloody Close would yer?

Joanne   At least I don't . . . –

Dave   Some leafy fuckin' cul-de-sac with its own piss-stained fuckin' Spar. Some two-up two-down with a plastic fuckin' playground out the back. Scrappin' over a bag o' soggy chips with the rest of the primates. That's what you all aspire to int it? Some wet God-awful nightmare of the Northern working class, yeah. I'm green with fuckin' envy I am, Joanne, yer've put yer finger on the button there, well done.

Joanne   So that's why you abandoned us is it?

Dave   We were dead already, Joanne, let's not get petty.

Joanne   What, were it not minimalist enough for yer?

Dave   The space between your ears, woman, yer know what I'm fuckin' talkin' about.

Joanne   Abandoned it, that house! After all we'd been workin' towards . . . –

Dave   We were finished, yer fuckin' idiot, I didn't have that choice!

Joanne   That's right, Dave, I remember.

Dave   'Abandon you'! Jesus Christ. I was suffocating up there!

Joanne   Come back home t' some note left on the mantelpiece. Some eight-year-old scrawl tellin' me t' move back in with me dad, yeah, that's really fuckin' petty.

Dave   It were over between us anyway, yer know that!

Joanne   Ten years I've been waitin' on you, David Harrison.

Dave   Yeah, and it's taken me ten years just to even try and rectify some of the damage . . .

Joanne   F' me to absolve you, yer mean.

Dave   F' me to look you in the face. F' me to try and make sense of all the effort I made . . .

Joanne   The effort you made?

Dave   All the effort it took me to just get out the bed of a morning. The effort to look the woman I loved in the face and not feel like I have to batter the bloody sense into her. – Are yer listening?

Joanne   Yeah.

Dave   Because I look into the future and all I see is shit. I take every possible outcome given who I am and what I do, and all the fucking maybes and small talk on that piece of shit bastard sofa – the one you forced me to buy on our account I might add, another fuckin' five years' worth of interest. Interest we'd still be payin' off t' this day, Joanne, don't pretend yer don't know. – You know, it's written all over yer, it was just like everythin' else. The sofa, the car, the house, the fuckin' never-endin' wardrobe upstairs. Working my arse off t' support some life that I were never even fit for, that were rotten with the stink o' dead babies. The babies we aborted. The babies we postponed, Joanne. The ones dependent on my solvency, the ones I had you murder. — Oh, don't worry, I 'ant forgot. How the fuck could I? I've been strugglin' t' face up t' that promise since I first caught the train straight out o' that moronic arsehole of a town. The years n' months together, those three little bastards. This woman who wanted the world and everything in it, but who could never stand accountable because she couldn't decide what the fuck she was supposed to with it all anyway. Jesus Christ, I should've left you in a shot had I had more sense, had I not listened to you and owned up to my own financial inadequacy. Oh, that is what you called it eventually though int it? The inadequate, the bankrupt? — Had we not been so dependent on the little income that we actually had that the very idea of separation meant death. Stuck in that house for five years, while I'm staring into this never-ending vacuum and deludin' myself like every other wanker out there, that what? That democracy makes me special? That because I'm not born in some East African fuckin' village somewhere, that I'm somehow entitled to my success? That with hard work and perseverance alone I could be one of a thousand other people than the fat lonely bastard that I really am. Jesus Christ, what was I thinkin'? Wavin' around some English degree that never got me anywhere. Job after miserable job, dependent on some miracle, some mythical promotion that never fuckin' happened, that were never going to happen, that I 'ant got the talent for, Joanne, let's face it. The weeks and months just slippin' through my fingers, while you, in your Buddha-like compassion, continue to spend and you spend and you spend and you spend. The handbags and the shoes. Booking fucking holidays behind my back while I'm cracking my brain open just t' make up the minimum payments, and for what? For a life that was always going to be beyond us. For a life that was always going to pass us by. For a life built on credit cards and debit schemes, this towering fuckin' inventory of plastic, of borrowed goods and lowered interest rates, and consolidated fuckin' repayment plans that they threw at us like sweets, the bastards. The dirty, unaccountable bastards. The voice on the end of the phone who offers yer the world if yer only prepared to pay for it later. And that I could never repay! And that I built n' furnished your house with, Joanne, and

who I killed your children with, and that you, like a dunce, placed
into my trust. – And what? Yer think that didn't take some effort?
You think you were the only one? You think that all the promises
you bullied me into . . . ?

Joanne   The promises you broke, yer mean.

Dave   That I can't even cut it as a human fuckin' being. D'yer
want t' know how that feels?

Long pause.

I was thinkin' of hangin' myself.

Joanne   Were yer?

Dave   I was thinkin' of doin' that, Joanne, yeah.

Joanne   Oh.

Dave   I thought I'd explained all that in my letters.

Pause.

Joanne   Oh, right.

Dave   It's despicable, I know.

Pause.

Joanne . . . –

Joanne   No, it is despicable, yer right.

Dave   I mean . . . –

Joanne   D'yer know how long it's took us just to make the
minimum payments?

Pause.

D'yer know that, Dave, d'yer?

Dave   No, I . . . –

Joanne   To consolidate each and every one of your fuck-ups so I'm not doped up on pharmaceuticals year on in? D'yer know how long that takes?

Pause.

Why d'yer think my dad's still workin' 'is arse off at sixty-fuckin'-five? What else d'yer think that shop's still payin' for, eh?

Pause.

D'yer even think about what it takes to admit that yer husband's not comin' home? To stand there like a scrounger and admit that he'd rather be anywhere else but here, with me? Have you any idea what that takes?

Pause.

Shall I tell yer how many men I've slept with since you left?

Dave   Oh . . . –

Joanne   It's not like I 'ant had the choice.

Pause.

Dave   No, thanks.

Long pause.

Thanks, that's . . . –

Joanne   Oh, yeah I spent it alright.

Dave   What, sorry?

Joanne   I spent it because you let me, Dave.

Pause.

Dave   Oh . . . –

Joanne   Because I were too fuckin' young t' know any different.

Long pause.

Stood there wi'yer Chardonnay and yer endangered fuckin' species.

Dave   Look, Joanne . . . —

Joanne   I think yer'd better get yerself cleaned up don't you?

Dave   I mean.

Long pause.

I mean, if yer'd just let me . . . —

Joanne   Clean it up f' fucksake, yer makin' me feel sick.

Long pause.

He exits into the bathroom, shutting the door behind him.

He switches on the bathroom light and moves straight to the sink.

He checks his scars in the mirrors on the bathroom cabinet.

Pause.

He turns on the taps and fills up the sink with hot water, still checking his scars.

Once the sink is filled, he turns the taps off.

Pause.

He hesitates.

Pause.

He proceeds to wash his face.

As he does the above, **Joanne** *slowly straightens herself out – her clothes, hair, etc.*

Long pause.

Joanne *pulls herself up off the futon, and moves to the kitchen area.*

She gulps down some wine from the wine glass.

Pause.

She hesitates.

Pause.

She reaches for her cigarettes.

Pause.

She puts the cigarettes down.

She hesitates.

Pause.

She picks up the CD and takes it out of its case.

Pause.

She takes the CD, her wine and her cigarettes, and moves to the office area.

She sits down.

Pause.

She switches on the laptop, and places the CD in its compartment.

Long pause.

She clicks the mouse.

Long pause.

She clicks the mouse.

Long pause.

She double-clicks the mouse.

Pause.

Sam Cooke's 'A Change is Gonna Come' begins to play from the laptop.

Joanne *peers through the blinds, looking out of the window, listening.*

As she does this . . .

Dave – *washed and dried – exits the bathroom, and enters the living space.*

He hesitates.

Pause.

He enters the bedroom.

Pause.

He hesitates.

Pause.

He moves to the bedside cabinet, and, sitting on the bed, rummages through it.

He digs out his chequebook.

Pause.

He rummages through the cabinet.

Pause.

He finds a pen.

Pause.

He writes a cheque.

Long pause.

He tears the cheque out of the chequebook.

Pause.

He hesitates.

Pause.

He stands up and, taking the cheque with him, leaves the bedroom.

He moves through the living area and into the kitchen area.

Pause.

He takes the wine bottle.

He fills up the wine glasses with the remaining wine.

As he does this . . .

Joanne, *sitting in the office area, turns the music's volume down.*

Pause.

She lights another cigarette.

Pause.

Dave *takes one of the wine glasses.*

Holding the wine glass, and the cheque, he hesitates.

Long pause.

Dave *makes to move to* **Joanne**, *when . . .*

Joanne   I'll happily have his dinner on the table.

Dave   Who?

Long pause.

I'll happily have his dinner on the table.

Dave   Who?

Joanne   I'll iron his shirts.

Pause.

I'll iron his shirts and his socks. I'll cook his dinner, wash his pots.

Pause.

I'd give anything, Dave. Really I would.

She stubs her cigarette out.

Long pause.

She peers through the blinds.

It comes back.

Long pause.

I said it comes back.

Dave   Sorry, what?

Joanne   Yer accent.

Dave   Oh . . . –

Joanne   When yer get mad. Yer accent creeps back.

Dave   Oh, right.

Long pause.

Dave *puts the cheque and the wine glass down on the kitchen counter.*

He sits on one of the stools.

He sips from his own glass of wine.

Long pause.

Joanne *turns away from the blinds and stands.*

Pause.

She moves to the kitchen area.

Pause.

She takes her glass of wine and sips from it.

Pause.

She puts her wine glass on the counter, then strokes **Dave***'s hair, moving it away from his brow.*

Long pause.

Joanne *moves behind the counter.*

She starts clearing up the mess on the kitchen counter – clearing up the chorizo and putting it in the bin, returning the ingredients to the cupboards, washing down the chopping board, straightening up, etc.

Long pause.

Joanne (*as she cleans up*)   I mean.

Pause.

I mean if there's somethin' . . .

Pause.

She hesitates.

Dave *climbs off the kitchen stool, and . . .*

Joanne   I mean, if yer'd really I didn't . . . –

Dave *grabs* **Joanne** *from behind.*

Joanne   Ow! Jesus Christ! . . . –

Dave *pulls down* **Joanne**'s *tracksuit bottoms and underwear.*

Joanne   Jesus Christ, Dave.

Dave *drags his own trousers and pants down.*

Joanne   Dave, please yer don't have to . . . –

Dave *fucks* **Joanne** *against the kitchen counter.*

Joanne   Alright.

Dave *fucks* **Joanne** *against the kitchen counter.*

Joanne   Alright, just . . . –

Dave *fucks* **Joanne** *against the kitchen counter.*

Time passes.

Dave *stops, catches his breath.*

Pause.

Dave *fucks* **Joanne** *against the kitchen counter.*

Time passes.

Dave *stops, catches his breath.*

Pause.

Joanne *helps* **Dave**, *reaching between their legs, and guiding his penis.*

Dave *fucks* **Joanne** *against the kitchen counter.*

A long time passes.

Dave *stops, catches his breath.*

Long pause.

Dave *pulls up his trousers and pants.*

He grabs his glass of wine, and marches to the bedroom.

He enters the bedroom, slamming the door behind him.

He sits on the bed.

Long pause.

Joanne *pulls up her underwear and tracksuit bottoms.*

Long pause.

She sips her wine.

Pause.

She hesitates.

Pause.

She moves across the living space and stops by the bedroom door.

Pause.

She knocks lightly on the bedroom door.

Joanne *opens the bedroom door and enters.*

Joanne (*as she enters*)   Yer don't have to lock yerself away.

Dave   No, really . . . –

Joanne   It's not a problem.

She sits on the bed, next to **Dave**.

Very long pause.

Joanne   I could get used t' this place.

Dave   Could yer?

Long pause.

Yeah, well . . . –

Joanne   Stupid old cunt.

Dave   No, that's . . .

Very long pause.

Thought of any names yet?

Joanne   Sorry?

Dave   Any names?

Very long pause.

Joanne *gets up off the bed, and moves to the bedroom window.*

She opens the blinds.

Pause.

She peers through the window.

Pause.

She grabs the window and wrenches it open.

The noise of the streets below.

She leans out of the window, looking out at the opposite flats.

Long pause.

Dave *puts his wine down, and stands.*

He moves across to **Joanne**, *standing behind her.*

Dave *and* **Joanne** *look out the window.*

Very long pause.

Dave *puts his hand round* **Joanne**'s *waist.*

Lights fade.

Juicy Fruits

Juicy Fruits was first performed at Òran Mór, Glasgow, on 17 October 2011, as one of five plays produced by Òran Mór and Paines Plough which then toured to Edinburgh, Manchester and Coventry, with the following cast and creative team:

Nina	Denise Hoey
Lorna	Clare Waugh
Kev/Barista	Ben Winger

Director George Perrin
Design Kirsten Hogg
Lighting Tim Deiling
Sound Scott Twynholm

>

Characters

Nina, *thirties*
Lorna, *thirties*
Kev, *thirties*
Barista
Orang-Utan

The same actor can play the Barista and Kev.
The same actress can play Lorna and the Orang-Utan.

Settings

A coffee-shop, somewhere in a leafy area of a big city.
A small clearing in the jungles of Borneo.

One

The outside area of a big-brand coffee shop.

Day.

Lorna *is sitting at the table, sipping a peppermint tea.*

She gently rocks a pushchair. In the pushchair is her baby son, who is sleeping.

Nina *has just arrived and is sitting at the table with a large latte and a pastry.*

A **Barista** *is close by, clearing up the empties from another table. Throughout the scene, until indicated, he potters in and out of the scene (where appropriate), keeping an eye on* **Nina** *and* **Lorna**'s *table.*

Nina   Are you sure I can't get you anything? A pastry?

Lorna   No, really, I'm fine.

Nina   Ah, you're watching your weight.

Lorna   We've already eaten, I mean.

Nina   Oh, okay.

Lorna   We actually ate before we left, I like to give him his lunch at home. It's part of his whole . . .

Nina   His routine.

Lorna   Yes, and I don't really like to . . .

Nina   Break it.

Lorna   Break it, no. It's better for his naps, it's better he knows . . .

Nina   It's better he has some kind of routine. Don't worry, I'm way ahead in the child-rearing department, you know they're not actually that different to monkeys.

Lorna   Well, it's better for everyone really.

Nina   I expect it helps his brain to grow. Oh, he's a sweetheart, isn't he?

Lorna   He's fast asleep, thank God.

Nina   He's a sweetheart, Lorna, really. Arrr, look at his chubby little cheeks.

Lorna   Yes, I know, it's the formula.

Nina   And he's so fucking trendy. Look at his little blazer, look.

Lorna   It's H&M. That and the V-neck.

Nina   I could quite go for him with a bit of stubble, bless.

Lorna   Well, you only just missed him having one of his tantrums.

Nina   Oooh, were you having a tantrum, Samson, were you?

Lorna   Yes, he practically cleared the table next to me.

Nina   Were you kicking and screaming, yes? Oh yes you were . . .

Lorna   Not that I can blame him of course. Poor little thing's been up since five o'clock.

Nina (*to Samson*)   Five o'clock! Five o'clock!

Lorna   And he doesn't usually sleep in the Maclaren to be fair. Not when he can help it anyway, I don't think he likes to miss out on any of the action.

Nina   Arrr, he's beautiful really.

Lorna   Thanks.

Nina   He's really beautiful, Lorna, well done.

Lorna   Well, it wasn't . . .

Nina   No, really, well done.

Lorna   Well, it wasn't anything . . .

Nina   He's got your chin.

Lorna   Has he?

Nina   He's got your jawbone, oh definitely. I mean, it's so pronounced.

Lorna   I thought he'd have more hair.

Nina   Did you?

Lorna   Well, you know.

Nina   You've got fantastic hair, it's so thick.

Lorna   It's actually going grey.

Nina   Tell me about it, my God! Have you been using any products?

Lorna   No, not since Samson, not for a good few . . .

Nina   Years?

Lorna   I was going to say months.

Nina   Well, I haven't since I left the jungle, it's driving me insane.

Lorna   I was hoping to treat myself.

Nina   You should definitely treat yourself.

Lorna   I think there's a Boots down the high street, you know we could . . .

Nina   Boots, yes, definitely. Are you sure you won't have a bite of this?

Lorna   No, really, I'm fine.

Nina   Have a bite, go on, you'll be doing me a favour.

Lorna   No, I shouldn't really . . .

Nina   Take half, go on. Go on, take half of it, Lorna, please. I can't bear the thought of having to jog it all off tomorrow morning.

I mean I shouldn't have gone and bought it at all, I'm like some obese fucking nutter or something.

Lorna   Oh rubbish.

Nina   No, I'm deadly serious, I'm . . . deadly serious.

Lorna   But you're as thin as a rake, Nina. Christ, I wish I had your figure.

Nina   You wish.

Lorna   Sorry?

Nina   You wish you could see me balancing on the weighing scales some mornings in the nude. Just look at this tummy, look.

Lorna   And there's a lot of men who find that sort of thing quite attractive.

Nina   The worst thing was I actually felt sorry for it. All alone like it had lost it's mummy or something, the last little pastry left to fend for itself – I mean, who does that, Lorna? You know I bought a pack of envelopes the other day they seemed so lonely up there on the shelf.

Lorna   Well, I'd say you need to put a few pounds on if anything, you're practically wasting away.

Nina   Honestly. I've been all over the place since I got back. I can hardly remember what day it is, never mind . . .

Pause.

Never mind the . . . the . . .

For a moment, the sound of the rainforest swells and engulfs the stage (and **Nina**'s *thoughts).*

We hear the beginnings of an Indonesian Dayak chant, until . . .

Lorna   Well, it's great to see you.

Nina   It's great to see you too, Lorna, God. You and the little one.

Lorna   When you called me on the . . .

Nina   You and the little bundle, Christ, I didn't expect him to be so big already. How old is he now?

Lorna   Eight months.

Nina   No.

Lorna   He'll be one in January, I know.

Nina   One, wow, that's the first number after zero. Where does the time . . . ?

Lorna   Where does it go, Nina, exactly. You know I couldn't believe it when Adrian said you'd called. I thought you'd be still off on one of your adventures.

Nina   Life is an adventure, Lorna.

Lorna   Yes, he said that you'd called a couple or so times and, you know, I couldn't quite believe it was actually . . .

Nina   And it's time we caught up, don't you think?

Lorna   Oh, absolutely. Absolutely, Nina, yes.

Nina   I mean, I can't even remember the last time we . . .

Lorna   Six years ago.

Nina   No.

Lorna   Six years ago, and it was at Danny's wedding.

Nina   Danny's wedding, you're right. God, that was bloody boring wasn't it? All that church shit.

Lorna   He's got a boy now.

Nina   Oh, has he? Wow.

Lorna   He's got a two-year-old boy, him and Janine.

Nina   Janine! – Yes, that's right, and you were still with Justin..

Lorna   Was I?

Nina   Yes, you were, you were all over him, you little tart.

Lorna   Well, I must have been arseholed.

Nina   Oh, you were arseholed alright.

Lorna   Well, we all were back . . .

Nina   No, but you were paralytic, Lorna, come on. – And, God, he was a waste of space, wasn't he?

Lorna   Who?

Nina   Justin. He was something of a microbe, Lorna, really.

Lorna   Well, yes, I . . .

Nina   He was a microbe, admit it.

Lorna   Yes, I suppose . . .

Nina   I mean, honestly. A microbe.

Lorna   He was a brilliant guitarist.

Nina   Well, he's no Carlos Santander I'll give him that. Did you know he flashed my sister?

Lorna   He did what?

Nina   He flashed my sister during the service. There's no wonder you had a drink problem.

Lorna   I didn't have a drink problem.

Nina   Well, your Aiden sounds nice.

Lorna   Who?

Nina   Aiden.

Lorna   Adrian.

Nina   Well, your Adrian sounds nice.

Lorna Yes, he is nice, thank you.

Nina I thought he sounded lovely on the phone.

Lorna No, he is.

Nina Sort of sexy. Deep and sort of chocolately . . .

Lorna He's had tonsillitis.

Nina Urrr.

Lorna Yes, I know.

Nina Urrr, God, I hate tonsillitis. I used to get it all the time when I was a kid.

Lorna Well, it's meant he's had to take time off work, which is kind of annoying . . .

Nina Yes, I know, and he should be gargling a cup of salt water at least five times a day. I suppose he's a guitarist too, is he? I always knew you'd end up with a guitarist.

Lorna Actually he's a barrister.

Nina Oh, well done.

Lorna Thanks, that's . . .

Nina Ker-ching.

Lorna Well, it . . . comes in handy, you know? I can't say I disapprove of being whisked away on a city break at a moment's notice. Venice or Barcelona or wherever.

Nina Well, if he ever needs a mistress . . .

Lorna No, I'll tell him that.

Nina And I bet he's proud of this one too, is he?

Lorna Oh yes.

Nina (*to Samson*) I bet he's proud of you, you funny little fanny magnet you.

Lorna   Yes, he's been fantastic.

Nina   I bet he is, yes.

Lorna   He's been so . . .

Nina (*in an 'accent'*)   Yo, he da man, bitch.

Lorna   Well . . . Well, they can't seem to get enough of each other to tell you the truth.

Nina   A daddy's boy.

Lorna   Yes, he's been feeding him the bottle from day one. The formula, I mean.

Nina   You can tell he's going to be a boy.

Lorna   I mean, I wasn't particularly keen to start him off right away.

Nina   Oh, weren't you?

Lorna   Not right away, no. I imagined I'd keep him on breast milk for the first six months at least. For the goodness, I mean.

Nina   For the goodness, yes. Yes, Lorna, the goodness.

Lorna   Build up his immune system. That's what they tell you anyway, the midwives.

Nina (*picks up her coffee, sips*)   Oh well, I'm sure he's alright.

Lorna   He just wouldn't latch on.

Nina   He wouldn't what?

Lorna   He wouldn't latch on to my nipple.

Nina (*puts her coffee down*)   Urrr, really?

Lorna   No, he couldn't get his mouth around them.

Nina (*wiping her mouth with the napkin*)   Oh, he couldn't, could he?

Lorna   Well, either that or he didn't want to. Or . . .

Nina   Mm, yes.

Lorna   Or it was something I was doing wrong. You know, I actually felt like I was going to die the couple of times he did manage it. The pain . . .

Nina   The pain, yes, I bet.

Lorna   And you're producing all this milk that you can't do anything with.

Nina   Don't forget your pastry.

Lorna   For days this went on at first, the two of us in this ongoing battle, and the midwives contradicting each other all the time.

Nina   Cunts.

Lorna   Yes, so we had no choice but to switch to the formula in the end. I mean thank God for Adrian really, it was him who convinced me in the end. It just seemed like such a waste of effort. A waste of effort, and a waste of energy more importantly. Sterilising the bottles, sterilising the steriliser, keeping the milk at the right temperature . . .

Nina   Keeping the milk at the right temperature.

Lorna   It's just that feeling of powerlessness that kills me. We did try and use the breast pump for a while, but he just didn't . . .

Nina   Latch on.

Lorna   He just didn't take to it for some reason.

Nina   Your nipple, yes, we established that – I doubt it's anything unusual.

Lorna   And of course the guilt that comes with that.

Nina   Oh, but you shouldn't beat yourself up.

Lorna   The guilt that comes with everything, Nina. I mean, okay, he's been on solids for a few weeks now, but . . . but even with the food, it seems he only wants to eat it when his dad . . .

Nina   They're very close then.

Lorna   And it's wonderful of course, to see that bond, to . . . to see them both . . .

Nina   I'm sure they all go through phases, don't they? I fucking hated my stepmother when I was growing up. There were times when I could have knifed her in the face.

Lorna   It really does change everything.

Nina   Oh, but that's how life works surely? The plants, the rivers, the trees . . .

Lorna   No, but, really, the physical act of childbirth, Nina. It really wipes it out of you, you know? I mean he's nearly a year now and I'm still taking tablets for my blood pressure that's through the fucking roof, can you believe that? Not to mention the whole psychological . . .

Nina   The responsibility.

Lorna   The endless toil. The psychological, emotional, physiological . . .

Nina   Responsibility.

Lorna   The day-to-day grind that's forever built around his bloody mealtimes.

Nina   Of course.

Lorna   And does he give me any thanks for it?

Nina   He doesn't, no.

Lorna   And why should he, Nina?

Nina   Well, no.

Lorna   Not to mention these tablets and my fucking blood pressure going off the radar . . .

Nina   Modern medicine, it's just such bollocks though isn't it really?

Lorna   I mean, it's just become so hard to have any perspective, to . . . sit here and have an intelligent conversation. Even Adrian won't . . .

Nina   Adrian sounds smoochy.

Lorna   What?

Nina   Adrian sounds smoochy.

Lorna   He does what, sorry?

Nina   He's a smoochy smoocher.

Pause.

Lorna   Oh, for Christ's sake, Nina . . .

Nina   What? Come on, do you think I came all this way to watch you cry into your prune juice?

Lorna   It's peppermint tea.

Nina   Well, that's not the Lorna I know. You've got a beautiful baby boy f' Christ'sake, you think I can't see that? – I mean, I'm sure it's really 'woah' and everything, but just who . . . who the fuck is this woman anyway, Lorna, hm? Who is this fucking woman?

Pause.

Sorry, no, that was wrong of me. I didn't mean for it to come out like that. You know my head's still in the jungle? It's funny, but I can't seem to . . .

For a moment, the sound of the rainforest swells and engulfs the stage (and **Nina**'s *thoughts*).

We hear the beginnings of an Indonesian Dayak chant, until . . .

Lorna   No, that's fine, I understand.

Nina   I'm finding it hard to relate to human beings at the moment.

Lorna   Six years.

Nina   Six years, yes. And the pace of life here, God, everyone's so stuck-up and . . . fucking precious about everything. – Hey, you know what I think we should do?

Lorna   I think we should just try our best to be content, don't you?

Nina (*in an accent*)   Hey, let's get wasted, man.

Lorna   What, sorry?

Nina (*in an accent*)   Let's get wasted and do some drugs, man.

Lorna   Ha, well you've certainly still . . .

Nina   No, but seriously, I've got a dealer living in the flat above me. I bet I could easily pick up a bit of whatever it is the kids are taking these days – Hey, you know I'm in Bethnal Green now? Can you believe I'm actually living next door to a mosque? I mean, God, the whole street could explode any minute.

Lorna   Well, that must be different. Exciting.

Nina   Oh, it is exciting, you're right, it's nothing like round here. Just me and my sister and her stepbrother and his friend . . .

Lorna   And your dealer.

Nina   And my sexy black dealer and the noise of the Friday morning prayers . . . You know, I expect you'd probably hate it.

Lorna   Oh, I expect I probably would.

Nina   Yes, and it's funny because if there's one thing I've learned from my travels it's that we're all so vastly different. Racially, culturally and intellectually . . .

Lorna   Well I'd certainly love to hear about Borneo.

Nina   Oh my God, it was amazing!

Lorna   Oh, really? Because, you know I can't imagine . . .

Nina   Totally mind-blowing.

Lorna Well, then you'll have to tell me, it sounds . . .

Nina Life-changing, Lorna. I mean . . .

Lorna It sounds like another world.

Nina To see a whole species on the brink of extinction. Amazing!

Lorna Amazing.

Nina It's just so fucking amazing. – Oh, and I just have to show you the tribe.

Lorna Who?

Nina The tribe, the Dayak tribe. – That's who we stayed with, I mean, at the reserve, they're actually . . .

She gets out her purse.

They're actually practising cannibals.

Lorna Oh, really?

Nina Honestly, Lorna, they're just so fucking uncivilised, look. Here . . .

She opens her purse and shows **Lorna** *a photo.*

Nina Here's a picture of me with one of them there.

Lorna Oh. Oh, well, he's . . .

Nina Odem.

Lorna Oh them what, sorry?

Nina No, Odem. Odem, that's his name, he's one of the tribal leaders.

She takes the photo out of her purse and passes it to **Lorna**.

Nina I mean, it just changes your perspective on everything really.

Lorna Oh, he's got no clothes on, look.

Nina   He has got no clothes on, you're right. There's actually a real spirituality to the place if the truth be told. To the jungle, I mean. The jungle and the natives and the whole way of living that's just so natural and spontaneous and kind of wild. — To be honest, I think you'd probably hate it out there too.

Lorna   Well, I suppose if you've got nothing on.

Nina   Hm?

Lorna   If you haven't got a job or a house or an education or whatever. Tell me, how is Kevin anyway? Has he still got his dreadlocks?

Nina   Kevin's dead.

Lorna   He's what, sorry?

Nina   Well, he's not actually dead.

Lorna   Oh . . .

Nina   He's just kind of dead.

Lorna   Oh God, he's not sick is he?

Nina   No, he's just spiritually and emotionally redundant.

Lorna   Oh, but you two . . .

Nina   He's still out there actually.

Lorna   Still out there?

Nina   Yes, he's . . . running around after rhinos or whatever.

Lorna   But I don't understand, you two were just so perfect together . . .

Nina   Yes, and we're having coffee.

Lorna   What?

Nina   We're having coffee, Lorna, it's been six years. — I mean, Christ, let's go and see a band or something, let's get away from this fucking rat race.

Lorna   But we're not even in the rat race.

Nina   I mean, you can't be a stay-at-home mum all your life, Lorna, it's . . . it's just been such a desperately long time hasn't it? I feel like I hardly know you.

Lorna   Yes, and you're right, it is great that we've finally . . .

Nina   It's been so fucking long, Lorna, please, one night.

Lorna   Of course one night of course.

Nina   One night this weekend or something, come on.

Lorna   Well, I should probably check with Adrian. Let me speak to . . .

Nina   I'll speak to Adrian.

Lorna   Well, I don't know . . .

Nina   I'll speak to Adrian, alright? You know he'll listen to me.

Lorna   What do you mean 'he'll listen to you'? You've never even . . .

Nina   Yes and I just said I would didn't I? Jesus Christ, Lorna, forget about the sprog for five minutes, do yourself a favour.

Lorna   Take my mind off what?

Nina   Take your mind off the sprog f' fuck's sake. – I mean, wouldn't he rather be with his dad anyway?

Lorna   You know I'm beginning to think I should never have answered your . . .

Nina   Oh fuck off, you were desperate to answer my call.

Lorna   What?

Nina   Sat there like Mother Goose.

Lorna   I'm nothing like Mother Goose.

Nina   You're exactly like Mother Goose. I could see you from half a mile down the street when I was on my way up here just now. – And do you know how long it's taken me?

Lorna   Alright, now, just . . .

Nina   One bus and two train rides, Lorna, one bus and two fucking train rides. And I've sat here and listened to your stories while you gobble up my croissant.

Lorna   Gobble up? I haven't even touched your croissant!

Nina   You and your mochaccinos and your traffic lights and your Twitter. – What, aren't you even a little bit interested in the orang-utans at least?

Lorna   Excuse me?

Nina   You haven't once asked me about the orang-utans.

Lorna   Well, all right then . . .

Nina   Don't you dare ask me about them now.

Long pause.

There's some photos in my bag if you're interested.

Lorna   There's what?

Nina   The orang-utans, look, don't move.

Lorna   But . . .

Nina   Don't move I said, let me . . .

She clumsily reaches into her handbag and gathers together her photographs.

Let me get to them a minute, I'm . . .

Lorna   Oh, Nina, please, this is so . . .

Nina (*to the photos*)   Come on come on f' fuck's sake . . .

Lorna   You know this really isn't exactly how I'd planned . . .

Nina   Oh, here's Seamus.

Lorna   Who?

Nina   Here's Seamus, look.

She passes **Lorna** *a photograph.*

Pause.

Nina   Well, aren't you going to . . . ?

Lorna   Oh, 'Seamus', I see.

Nina   He's one of the baby orphans.

Lorna   Oh, is he?

Nina   Yes, I named him myself.

Lorna   Well, I'm sure he's . . .

Nina   I actually think he looks like Seamus Heaney. Don't you think he looks like Seamus Heaney?

Lorna   Well, he is very cute I suppose.

Nina (*of the baby*)   He's cuter than that thing.

Lorna   What?

Nina   Yes, and he was actually one of three. The others were shipped to China after they killed their mother.

Lorna   Who killed their mother?

Nina   I know, it's dreadful isn't it? – Yes, the poachers, they . . . they shot the mother in the back of the head with their rifles, like . . . like, kabam!, you know? Blood everywhere, and the body just becomes this . . . moving mass of maggots within about a day, which is kind of traumatic for Seamus here. – I mean, you wouldn't believe how much they fetch on the black market. The babies, I mean. They cage them up and sell them to rich businessmen's wives, and the government are happy because they need the rainforest cleared for logging.

Lorna   What, and it's your job to . . . ?

Nina   It's our job to make life difficult for them, correct. To catch and protect the ones that got away, and to generally help conserve the surrounding environment, which is, as a matter of fact, about a hundred and fifty million years old.

Lorna   So you're really actually . . . ?

Nina   Yes, I am making a difference, you're right. — Here, that's the two of us at the refuge, look.

She passes **Lorna** *another photograph.*

Nina   Seamus and me. I really like that one.

Lorna   Yes, it's . . .

Nina   It's come out really well, I think.

Lorna   Yes . . . Yes, well you must . . .

Nina *passes* **Lorna** *a third photograph.*

Lorna   You must tell me all about them, Nina.

Nina   And here are all the other volunteers. They're all really decent people, you know?

Lorna   Oh, are they?

Nina   Yes, well you'd have to be, wouldn't you? I'd actually say you should come out and meet them if I didn't think you'd totally freak out at all the spiders and leeches and everything.

Lorna   Hm. Well, perhaps you can tell me all about it when we . . . ?

Nina   And there's another one. Me and the flying lemurs, look.

She passes **Lorna** *a fourth photograph.*

Lorna   Yes, the flying lemurs, look.

Pause.

Yes, I see you there now.

Nina   And another one.

Lorna   What?

Nina *passes* **Lorna** *a fifth photograph.*

Nina   And another one, look. More flying lemurs. You can keep it if you'd like.

Lorna   No, of course. I'd love to, just . . .

Nina   Take your pick, Lorna, go on. I can see you're –

She throws a photograph at **Lorna.**

Nina   – clearly impressed.

Lorna   What, are you . . . ?

Nina *throws a photograph at* **Lorna.**

Lorna   For Christ's sake, Nina . . .

Nina *throws two or three more photographs at* **Lorna.**

Lorna   Just wait a second . . .

Nina   What?

She throws a photograph at **Lorna.**

Lorna   For God's sake, Nina!

Nina   What's wrong with you, what? I thought you were interested.

Lorna   Well, of course I am, I'm fucking –

Nina *throws a series of photographs at* **Lorna.**

Lorna   – fascinated, Nina, just stop doing that a minute will you?! – Nina, will you please stop?!

Long pause

Here, let me . . .

She gathers up the strewn photographs, while **Nina** *sips her coffee.*

Pause.

Dear God, you're like some . . .

Nina   I'm sorry, I don't . . . I don't actually know what came over me, I honestly think it's your face.

Lorna   What?

Nina   Your face, it's . . .

For a moment, the sound of the rainforest swells and engulfs the stage (and **Nina**'s *thoughts).*

We hear the beginnings of an Indonesian Dayak chant, until . . .

Lorna   Well, what about it? What about my fucking face?

She picks up the last of the photos and dumps them on the table.

Beat.

I mean, really, Nina . . .

Nina (*makes to leave*)   This milk's too cold.

Lorna   Hm?

Nina   No, the milk's too cold in my latte, they've given me cold milk. Do you want anything? Another coffee? Another pastry maybe?

Lorna   Well, I haven't actually . . .

Nina   Then you'd better get cracking then.

Lorna   I haven't actually finished my tea yet, Nina.

Nina   You don't want it to go stale.

Lorna   I don't care if it goes stale. – Look, you're the one who insisted . . .

Nina   Yes, because I know you're starving.

Lorna   Excuse me?

Nina   You're always fucking starving. You've got an addictive personality, Lorna, face it, it was the same with the drink problem.

Lorna   I did not have a drink problem!

She's said this a wee bit too loud, and looks round at her immediate surroundings, a bit embarrassed.

Beat.

Lorna   Look, Nina . . .

Nina   You know you should try and channel it in a positive direction or something.

Lorna   Well, if you'd let me get a –

Nina *quickly exits, taking their cups.*

Lorna   – word in edgeways, Nina, I might just actually . . .

A sound of crashing tables and chairs and shattered glass, offstage, as **Nina** *has clearly stumbled into and knocked over another customer's table.*

Nina (*off*)   Alright I'm fine, I'm fine, nobody panic!

Lorna *peers over her shoulder at the commotion for a moment, then looks back to her table.*

Long pause.

She looks to her baby, and gently rocks the pushchair.

Pause.

She stops rocking the pushchair.

A moment's deliberation.

Pause.

She places her napkin on top of the pastry.

Pause.

Deliberation.

Pause.

She fiddles under the napkin and breaks a piece of the pastry off.

She scoffs the pastry, and readjusts the napkin.

Pause.

She sips her tea.

Pause.

She looks to the baby and pulls the hood of the pushchair down.

Pause.

She peers offstage to see what **Nina** *is doing.*

Beat.

Lorna *pulls the pastry out from under the napkin and proceeds to scoff the whole thing.*

As she does this, the **Barista** *enters and, unnoticed by* **Lorna**, *proceeds to wipe down the table with a cloth.*

Pause.

Lorna *sees the* **Barista** *and, with her back to him, stuffs the pastry into her mouth.*

Pause.

The **Barista** *picks the plate up from the table.*

Barista   Excuse me, have you finished with this?

Lorna (*with her mouth full*)   Hmph.

She places the napkin on the plate.

The **Barista**, *holding the plate, peers into the pushchair.*

Barista   Arr, he's sweet.

Lorna (*with her mouth full, gesticulates*)   Hmph hmph.

The **Barista** *smiles and exits.*

With difficulty, she chews and swallows the pastry.

Pause.

She peers over her shoulder, trying to catch a glimpse of **Nina**.

Pause.

Deliberation, then . . .

Lorna *pulls* **Nina***'s chair towards her slightly.* **Nina***'s handbag hangs on the edge of the chair.*

Pause.

Lorna *peers into the bag.*

Beat.

She checks over her shoulder, then rummages inside the bag.

Pause.

She takes out **Nina***'s purse and looks inside. She can't see any money, but lots of scraps of paper and receipts.*

Pause, and **Lorna** *quickly puts the purse back in the bag.*

She then pulls out a self-help book called The Power of Now. *Sandwiched in the book is another pack of photographs.*

She spies and takes the photographs out of the pack and begins to flick through them.

Pause.

She studies the photographs, and can't quite believe what she sees.

Pause.

As she flicks through the photographs, **Nina** *re-enters, holding two small plates, each with a large piece of chocolate cake on it. As she speaks, she sits back down at the table, placing the plates* *down before them both, while* **Lorna** *continues looking at the photographs.*

Nina (*as she enters, to Lorna*)   Of course I wouldn't want to force you or anything. I just thought, what with now. What with everything we've been through and where we are now, and . . . and, God, I mean it's so important not to let old friendships just fizzle away like that, don't you think?

Lorna *is studying the photographs.*

Pause.

Nina (*seemingly oblivious to what* **Lorna** *is doing*)   Don't you think that, Lorna?

Lorna   Hm?

Nina   I said it feels like it hasn't been any time at all though, really.

Lorna   Oh, it is important, yes.

Nina   The two of us together, like . . .

Lorna (*putting the photographs down on the table*)   Yes, you're right, you're right.

Nina   Like Thelma and Louise or something, you know? – Us against the world, the fucking . . .

Lorna   The fucking 'man'.

Nina   The fucking man, man, right! – I mean, Christ, I'm getting goose pimples just thinking about it. Nina and Lorna out on the town for the first time in years and just . . . just doing whatever the hell we feel like for once.

Lorna   Yes, and if I wasn't so busy.

Nina   Hm?

Lorna   I'm just so dreadfully busy, Nina, you know what it's like.

Nina   Oh . . .

Lorna   You know what it's like though surely? Trying to balance work and taking care of the . . .

Nina   Taking care of number one?

Lorna   I mean, she is a sweetheart, Nina, really.

Nina   She's what, sorry? Who's a sweetheart?

Lorna   No, it's just . . .

She hands the photographs that she found in the handbag to **Nina***.*

Beat.

Nina   Oh.

Lorna   Sorry, I know I shouldn't have looked, but . . . you know?

Nina   Oh, she's quite ordinary.

Lorna   What?

Nina   I think she's quite ordinary looking.

Lorna   Oh . . .

Nina   If the truth be told, Lorna, yes. She's actually quite plain, don't you think?

Lorna   Well, I wouldn't . . .

Nina   She's not a patch on little Samson here.

Lorna   Does Kevin know you're here?

Nina   Who? – Oh Christ, no. No, I . . . I just needed a change of scenery, that's all.

Lorna   Oh, really?

Nina   Yes, I just woke up one morning and . . .

Beat.

Lorna   You woke up one morning and?

Nina   Well, I thought I'd jump on a flight.

Lorna   Which flight?

Nina   It doesn't matter which flight, the point is I'm here with you, Lorna, aren't I?

Lorna   Well, no, I'm not sure that is . . .

Nina   The point is we're sitting here together, you and I, and . . .

As she speaks, we see that her breasts begin lactating through her top.

And it's just wonderful because, you know? Because it feels like no time has passed at all, and that . . . despite everything, we're just the same old goofy pals aren't we?

Lorna   We're not the same old anything.

Nina   No, but deep down. Deep down, I mean.

Lorna   Yes, deep down, Nina, sorry. You know, I look in the mirror sometimes . . .

Nina   Well, you shouldn't be doing that.

Lorna   What?

Nina   You shouldn't go looking into mirrors with those wrinkles, Lorna, God. – I mean, God, I'm talking about hearts, aren't I? Our hearts, Lorna, come on. Deep down at the bottom of our . . .

She, then **Lorna**, *both notice that her breasts are lactating. Beat.*

Lorna   Oh Christ, Nina . . .

Nina   So, how was your pastry then, hm?

Lorna (*grabs a couple of napkins*)   Look, if you need . . .

Nina *snatches the napkins off* **Lorna**, *and frantically wipes her top dry.*

Nina (*as she does so*)   No, I'm asking the questions.

Lorna   What?

Nina   I'm asking the . . . the fucking questions now, Lorna, okay?

Lorna   Well, alright, if you . . .

Nina   Sat there rifling through my bag while I'm doing my best to get you out of the house for five minutes.

Lorna   While you're what, sorry? Look, I'm only trying . . .

Nina   Sherlock Holmes.

Lorna   Who?

Nina   Sherlock bloody Holmes. Oh, I know what you're doing alright. – So, how was your pastry then, Sherlock?

Lorna   Yes, and I've told you before . . .

Nina   So how was it anyway, you old fat galumphing old thieving old Sherlock? What, did it finally live up your high standards then, did it? You and this leafy middle-class nightmare you've dragged me out to in the middle of the week . . . Well, go on.

Lorna   Well go on what?

Nina   You've had your pastry, now eat the cake.

Lorna   Eat the cake?

Nina   Yes, the cake, the cake, look!

Lorna   Oh Jesus . . .

Nina   Eat the fucking cake, Lorna, come on.

She takes her spoon and starts eating her piece of cake.

Beat.

Lorna   Jesus, Nina, I'm really not that . . .

Nina   Try it, go on, it's delicious.

Lorna   No. No, really, I'm not too comfortable with . . .

Nina   But I just bought it for you, Sherlock.

Over the next, the **Barista** *re-enters with two steaming lattes.*
He places them on the table before **Nina** *and* **Lorna**, *then exits.*

Lorna   Look. I'm fine, really, thanks.

Nina   Well, I'm not going to eat it all by myself. – Here, let me race you.

Lorna   What?

Nina   Let me –

She starts frantically eating the cake as fast as she can.

– race you, you fucker, come on.

Lorna *watches* **Nina**.

Nina (*as she scoffs*)   Well, come on, Lorna, tuck in. Mmm, this is so . . .

She keeps eating as the **Barista** *re-enters with a small plate, on which is the bill.*

Barista   So, is everything all right for you, ladies?

Lorna   Yes, fine, . . . Fine, thank you.

Barista   Are you sure you wouldn't like anything else with that?

Lorna   No, that's . . .

Nina (*her mouth packed with cake*)   She'd like a blowjob.

Barista   Sorry, what?

Nina (*her mouth packed with cake*)   She actually needs a blowjob. I mean, her husband's obviously sick of the fucking sight of her by now, all his . . . pathetic attempts at flirting with me on the phone. Tell me, do you have any blowjobs on the menu? I mean, you look like you've got a tongue on you, mate, and I guarantee she'll only take two minutes to . . .

Lorna (*to the* **Barista**)   That's fine, thank you, yes.

The **Barista** *hesitates, then exits.*

Nina *continues scoffing the cake.*

Lorna *gently rocks the pushchair.*

Long pause.

Nina *finishes the cake, and wipes her mouth.*

Nina   Well, I win.

She sips her coffee.

Pause.

Nina   I said I win.

Lorna *inspects the bill.*

Pause.

She gets her purse and proceeds to place the money on the little plate with the bill.

Beat.

Lorna   Well, I suppose I don't mind paying this once . . .

Nina   It's my birthday next week.

Pause.

Lorna . . .

Lorna   Now, it was just the coffee and the cake wasn't it?

Nina   It's going to be my birthday this weekend. It's going to be my birthday, Lorna, and I'm . . . I'm petrified, Lorna, isn't that silly? Isn't that just so terribly silly though?

Pause.

Lorna   Oh.

Nina   I mean, we're really close aren't we?

Lorna   Well, yes . . .

Nina   But we're so very close, me and you. — What time do you finish?

Lorna   I don't 'finish'.

Nina   No, but what time do you finish work? – I mean, what time does he go to bed usually? – Christ, I'm so fucking tired.

Pause.

You know sometimes I'm not sure that we were put on this earth to be happy at all.

Pause.

Lorna, please . . .

Lorna   I can lend you thirty pounds.

Nina   Hm?

Lorna   Would thirty pounds help at all?

She takes the notes from her purse and hands them to **Nina**, *who hesitates . . .*

Lorna   Well, go on.

Nina *think. . . .*

Then takes the money.

Pause.

Lorna   You know you should speak to your parents if you're stuck. Haven't they always . . . ?

Nina   Fuck your money.

Lorna   Hm?

Nina   Fuck you and your money.

Lorna   Well . . . hasn't she got a name at least?

Nina   Hasn't who got a name?

She stuffs the photographs and the money in her handbag.

Pause.

Lorna *picks up the plate with the bill and makes to exit, then stops and turns back.*

Lorna   You could come and walk round the park with me.

Nina   What?

Lorna   No. I mean, if you want. A wee stroll by the pond or something?

Nina   Oh . . .

Lorna   It's just he needs another half hour's sleep, and I was going to . . .

Nina   Walk round the park.

Lorna   You see I'm actually rather lonely.

Nina   Oh?

Beat.

Oh, well that's –

She breaks into a little sardonic laugh or giggle.

– that's really disappointing, Lorna, thanks. 'Rather lonely'.

Lorna   Well, it's your choice, Nina.

She exits into the coffee shop with the bill, as **Nina** *continues to giggle.*

Pause.

Her giggles turn to tears.

She cries for a while, then . . .

The tears subside and she sits in limbo.

Long pause.

From out of the bag, she pulls a small tobacco tin which she places on the table in front of her.

She opens the tin and takes out a pre-rolled roll-up.

She sticks the roll-up in her mouth.

She goes to light it, when . . .

She looks at the baby in the pushchair.

Beat.

She goes to light it, when . . .

She looks again at the baby in the pushchair.

She hesitates.

Pause, then . . .

She grabs the pushchair and turns it round so the baby isn't facing her.

Beat.

She goes to light her roll-up, but . . .

Pause.

She puts the roll-up back in her tin.

Pause.

She deliberates.

Pause.

She takes the handle of the pushchair and starts to rock it.

This goes on for a few moments, her rocking getting a little bit faster, when . . .

Suddenly, the baby wakes, crying a little.

Beat.

She peers round at the baby.

She deliberates, and . . .

She rattles the pushchair.

No sound.

Beat.

She rattles the pushchair, harder this time.

No sound.

Beat.

She starts rattling the pushchair really hard this time, and . . .

The baby starts crying, which makes . . .

Nina *rock and rattle the pushchair even harder, and . . .*

The baby cries even louder, as . . .

The **Barista** *enters, carrying a tray. He sees what* **Nina***'s doing and . . .*

Barista   Whoa whoa whoa, are you sure you should be . . . ?

Nina *sees the* **Barista** *and violently pushes the pushchair at him.*

Barista (*catching the pushchair*)   Jesus Christ, woman, hey! —

Nina *grabs her things and quickly and exits, as . . .*

Barista (*to* **Nina**)   Hey, wait a minute, stop!

He races after **Nina***, exits, as . . .*

The baby's cries mutate into the shrill wails and cries of the Dayak tribe, as . . .

Two

The setting is transformed to the rainforest of Borneo.

Dusk.

The tail-end of a monsoon.

The sound of the chanting of the Dayak tribe fades, and the natural sounds of the rainforest swell.

In the thick of the jungle, **Nina***, now in her jungle outfit, is, with extreme effort (and difficulty) hanging/tying up a large sheet of canvas with ropes on to the branches of some trees.*

Her partner, **Kev***, also in jungle outfit, is sitting on the muddy ground, a distance from* **Nina***, holding a baby orang-utan, swaddled in a white blanket, in his arms, and feeding it with a bottle of milk.*

The loud noise of chanting and the previous baby crying gradually fade away as the scene is set, leaving only the natural sounds of the rainforest – animals, insects, the pitter-patter of the rain through the enormous trees.

Long pause.

Kev (*feeding the orang-utan*)   'Ey, Neens.

Pause.

'Ey Neens, look, she's dropping off.

Nina *continues working.*

Kev   The little one, look, she's going bye-bye finally.

Nina *keeps on working, heaving and grunting as she tussles with and snaps a few branches that are in her way.*

Kev   'Ere, Neens.

Pause.

Neens . . .

Nina   What, have you been telling her your life story, have you, Kevin?

Kev   Oh yeah, it's like *Great Expectations* over 'ere I reckon.

Nina   Well, try to leave out the bit about your old girlfriends, won't you? I don't want her slipping into a coma before the night's out, do you?

Kev   Oh, there's not much chance of that I don't think. Little cracker though, in't she? I reckon she's goin' to fit right in with the others back at lodge.

Nina   If we ever get to the lodge.

Kev   What d'yer mean 'if'? Of course we're goin' t'make it t'the lodge. There's nobody f' miles now, Nina, we're perfectly safe.

Nina   Right, and I'm sure that's what her mother thought before she was clubbed to death this morning.

Kev   Ah, come on, we don't know that, do we? She might be still out there for all we know.

Nina   Oh, really? So she just left her baby to die of malnutrition, did she? For Christ'sakes, Kev, I appreciate your optimism, but you know how quickly those bastards move, and once they realise the baby's been rescued . . .

Kev   Yeah, and then they'll 'ave me t'deal with won't they? Poachers my arse.

Nina   What?

Kev   Poachers my arsehole, Nina, I'm not frightened of them. (*To the orang-utan.*) We'll 'ave 'em cryin' like little girls won't we, Hendrix?

Nina   Who? – Oh, come on, you're not actually going to call her that, are you? Why do you have to be so cute all the time?

Kev   Who's being cute? I'm not fucking cute.

Nina   Well, alright, but you could at least try to be . . . Ah!

Kev   What?

Nina (*steps back from a tree*)   Ah, fuck!

Kev   Fuck, what is it?

Nina   Oh, fucking hell, a . . . a fucking centipede . . .

Kev   What, a . . . A centipede you mean?

Nina   Yes, Kevin, a centipede, a . . . Giant fucking centipede right there!

Kev   Oh man, that's shit. Shit, it didn't bite you did it?

Nina   No . . . No, it just came out at me from behind the tree, I think I'm . . .

She checks her hand and wrist.

Nina   I think it might have just been . . .

Kev   'Ey, I think you just woke her.

Nina   What?

Kev   Hendrix, look. I think yer just woke her. 'Ere look. (*To the orang-utan in a silly voice.*) Oh, 'ello. 'Ello there, little monkey, what are you doin' up? Did the silly woman frighten you, did she? Arrr, well never you mind. Never you mind about that now, my ginger fluff-pup, everything's going t'be just . . .

Nina   You're making me puke, you know that?

Kev   I'm what, sorry?

Nina   I said you're . . .

Kev   Making you puke?

Nina   Yes, and I've told you before not to talk like that. It turns my stomach when you do that, Kevin, you know it does.

Kev   Oh . . .

Nina   I didn't come back to listen you going on.

Kev   Oh, sorry like. What do you mean 'going on'?

Nina *goes to answer,*

Beat, then . . .

She thinks better of it, and continues building the camp.

Pause.

Kev   Did something happen to you over there? Back home, I mean.

Pause.

I mean, it's great yer back and everything, it's just . . .

Pause.

'Ere. Neens . . .

Nina *snaps more branches, purposefully ignoring* **Kev**.
Pause.

Kev   Yer look well sexy doin' that.

She continues, wilfully ignoring him.

Pause.

Kev (*making a joke*)   Aye, alright now, Tomb Raider, steady on . . .

Nina   I've got a job to do.

Kev   Yer've got what, sorry?

Nina   I've got to get this pitched for Christ's sakes, it's getting dark . . .

Kev   Well try not to injure yerself, will yer?

Nina *turns and gives him a 'look'.*

Beat.

Kev   Sorry, no . . .

Nina   You know, I am more than capable . . .

Kev   Oh, look, I was only sayin' . . .

Nina   Patronising cunt.

Kev   Eh? – Bloody 'ell, Nina, there's no need . . .

Nina   Well, if it's that bloody difficult then why don't you take over for a while?

Kev   Oh, gi' over, Nina, don't . . .

Nina   Put the tent up, Kevin, go on. Let's see how it's done.

Kev   See how it's done?

Nina   I mean, far be it for a woman to even attempt . . .

Kev   Oh, fuck off, you're just bein' daft now.

Nina (*goes to take the baby orang-utan*)   Yes, well, I do actually think we've got more important . . .

Kev *instinctively flinches. – they both take in the moment.*

Beat.

Nina   Oh, nice.

Kev (*pretending he didn't notice*)   What?

Nina   No, really. Nice.

Kev   Eh? What d'yer mean like?

Nina   Yes, that's really nice of you, Kev, thanks.

Kev   Oh, did you want . . . did you want to hold on to her or something, sorry?

Pause.

Kev   'Ere, Neens . . .

Nina   Look, it doesn't matter.

Kev   'Ey, come on now, sausage, yer know I didn't mean . . .

Nina   Just forget about it, okay? – (*Starts to move away.*) Yes, and I'm sure you didn't . . .

Kev   No, honestly like. I mean, I don't mind, Nina, it's . . .

Nina *breaks away from both* **Kev** *and the camp, and sits on a log a short distance apart, her back to him.*

Pause.

Kev   I guess we should probably start gettin' a move on anyway though, eh? Before it starts chuckin' it down, I mean.

With the orang-utan, he sidles towards **Nina** *as she is getting ready to spark her roll-up.*

Pause.

Kev   I mean, we 'ave still got another day's trek before we . . .

Nina *tries lighting her roll-up several times, but the lighter doesn't work.*

She throws the lighter into the bushes.

Long pause

Kev   We're making a real difference, Nina.

No answer.

Kev *goes to speak again,*

But doesn't.

Beat.

He looks to the baby orang-utan that is still in his arms.

You know I sometimes wonder what's going on in their heads like. Don't you ever do that? I know I do.

Pause.

Hold her for a bit if yer want.

He reaches out to touch **Nina**'*s shoulder, with* . . .

Kev   'Ere, Neens . . .

Nina *swats* **Kev**'*s hand like a fly.*

Pause.

Kev   Yeah.

Pause.

Yeah, well, I should probably get her out the rain.

Nina   Okay.

Kev   I mean, fuck knows how long she's been out here already, poor thing.

Pause.

Neens?

Pause.

Yeah, well, I'll just . . .

Nina   A nuclear bomb.

Kev   What, sorry?

Nina   A nuclear bomb.

Beat.

Kev   Oh. Oh, right . . .

Nina   If I could just get my hands on a single nuclear . . .

An audible rustling in the bushes.

Pause.

They look to each other.

Pause.

Kev *mimes 'Poachers'.*

Nina *gesticulates, 'What?'*

Kev *mimes 'Poachers. Over there, look. Shhh.'*

He carefully hands the baby orang-utan to **Nina***, and steps away towards the 'camp'.*

The noise of the rainforest sounds even more threatening than before, as . . .

Nina*, with the orang-utan, watches* **Kev** *as he picks up a shotgun which is with their camping gear.*

He takes the shotgun, and begins to load it, then . . .

Nina   Oh Christ, Kevin . . .

Kev   Sshhh.

He gesticulates to **Nina** *to take the orang-utan and move under/inside the Winnebago.*

Nina *nods, and both start to move in opposite directions.*

Pause.

Nina (*as she moves, almost whispered*)   You know I'm not sure . . . ?

A louder, more violent rustling in the bushes, and . . .

Fuck.

Kev *clicks the barrel of the shotgun shut and moves quickly towards the dense thickets . . .*

Nina (*almost whispered*)   Oh, fuck, Kevin, be –

Kev *disappears into the thickets.*

Nina   – careful will you? Shit!

The baby orang-utan is wriggling, beginning to grunt.

Oh . . . Oh, shit . . .

She tries to settle the orang-utan.

Shit, just . . .

She dithers, then moves away from the 'camp', across the muddy ground, and . . .

Sits down in a sheltered spot, (but one which is still open to the elements), and . . .

(*As she does so, to the orang-utan.*) Just calm down, alright? Just you . . . stay nice and . . .

She sits cross-legged, holding the baby orang-utan in her arms, and rocking it gently.

Sshhh, sshhh . . .

Very long pause.

She is rocking the baby orang-utan, as . . .

The noise of the rainforest settles down, but is still audible.

It feels much more peaceful.

Long pause, then . . .

There now.

Pause.

There now, that's my goodness. That's my good little goodness.

The orang-utan wriggles a bit, and . . .

She has a thought.

She checks her surroundings.

Pause.

She removes her top and bra.

That's my gorgeous goodness now, look. Come on . . .

She encourages the baby orang-utan to latch on.

Come on now, sweetheart, come on, it's only . . .

The baby orang-utan latches on to her boob.

Pause.

There. That's it. That's it now, my . . . Sshhh, what do we say? What do we say now, darling?

She peacefully breastfeeds the baby orang-utan, as . . .

A large adult female orang-utan enters, holding **Kev**'s *shotgun, and peering through the jungle thicket, behind and unseen by* **Nina**. *The adult orang-utan slowly approaches* **Nina** *from behind, as . . .*

Nina *sings 'You Are My Sunshine' to the baby orang-utan.*

Right behind her, the adult orang-utan, seeing her baby, raises the shotgun above **Nina**'s *head like a club.*

As **Nina** *sings the last line of the first verse of 'You Are My Sunshine'. . .*
The adult orang-utan swings the shotgun at **Nina**'s *head*

Blackout.

69

69, produced by Natural Shocks Theatre Company, was first performed at the Pleasance Courtyard on 1 August 2012 as part of the Edinburgh Festival Fringe, with the following cast and creative team:

A	Bella Heesom
B	Brett Fancy
C	Karen French
D	Ifan Meredith

Director Donnacadh O'Briain
Designer Signe Beckman
Lighting Ben Ormerod
Sound Nick Powell and Mark Cunningham
Producer Lucy Jackson

Characters

A, *female*
B, *male*
C, *female*
D, *male*

C He won't latch on.

D Give it time, be patient.

A Say something to him.

C Say something what?

D He just needs to hear your voice, darling. He needs to know everything's okay.

C Well, everything isn't okay. He's glaring at my tit like it's going to swallow him whole.

A You could sing him a song?

D Or perhaps not.

A Yes . . . or not.

C He's more interested in sucking his fingers, look. In and out, every two seconds, it's actually quite disgusting actually I think.

D Well, he's not gay.

C Excuse me?

D No . . . phallic, I mean. It's not . . . some sort of phallic demonstration or anything.

A Perhaps you could rub some chocolate on your nipple, dear?

D Look, I'm sure it's completely normal. He's only a day or two out of the womb, you can't expect him to . . .

A And he has to eat sometime.

D Exactly, yes, he's not going to starve.

C I wonder maybe they're too small. Maybe I'm too . . . flat-chested for him or something?

A Oh, nonsense.

C He keeps looking over at the woman in the bed there next to me. She's a double-D at least.

D   Oh, a double-D, really? What, the bed just there, you mean?

A   I still think you should think about some chocolate or ice cream maybe. You know if you were to just jiggle them around a bit.

C   Jiggle them around?

A   Yes, like in the shows, the what-you-call-it. The lap-dancers.

D   Burlesque.

A   Yes, the . . . burlesque lap-dancers, dear.

C   You mean, like tassles? I should decorate my nipples with tassles in the hope that he'll . . . ?

D   Well, I could think of worst things. He is his daddy's boy, after all.

C   He's dribbling.

D   He's thinking about it.

C   No, he's repulsed. He's clenching his little fists and he's repulsed. – Christ, am I really that foul? I thought this was supposed to be the most natural thing in the world.

B   No, she's perfect.
Christ, her face, she's . . .
She's so fucking dirty and she knows it, those lips.
What I could push between those lips, that beautiful thick red lipstick.
You know if I could just find one more picture . . . ?
Fuck, there must be something . . .
There must be some of her on holiday or something.
There must be something with her in a bikini or . . . or showing a bit of nipple at least.
Profile pictures, profile pictures . . . .
Ibiza, okay . . .
Okay, here we go.
Ah, that's better. That's much more . . . like it now, you . . .

Christ, you fucking inordinately dirty little bitch.
Oh, brilliant. Brilliant, wicked, that's just . . .

C   Are you alright in there, darling?

B   Yes, fine thanks, Mum!

C   Well, your dinner's going to be on the table in five minutes!

D   Of course he's masturbating.

C   What?

D   He's masturbating up there. On my laptop.

C   Oh for Christ's sakes, don't put it like that, Stephen, he's probably just . . .

D   Look between his fingers when he comes down.

C   He's probably just tweeting or twittering or whatever you call it.

D   No, he's definitely masturbating. My browser history's literally bursting with the stuff.

Look in the cracks between his fingers. The crust, the flakes . . . —

C   And how's your food, darling?

B   Yeah, I don't know. Fine, I suppose.

C   I was worried it was going to go cold. You were gone an awfully long time.

B   Oh, was I? Sorry, just . . .

C   There's kitchen roll if you need to wipe your hands. — So, is everything okay then?

B   Hm?

C   At school, I mean. You know your father and I were talking . . .

D   She talks too much.

C   Yes, and you don't talk at all, that's the reason we're in this fucking place, remember?

D   Well, perhaps if we'd do a little less talking and a little more fucking.

C   I've told you it's meaningless if I don't know how you feel.

D   Oh, 'how I feel', I'm standing there at the end of the bed with an erection for Christ's sakes.

C   No, but it's not normal.

D   What's not normal?

C   No, I'm not normal, I mean, I'm not normal. – Look . . .

B   Look, I know it sounds weird, but when I take a shit?

A   What, you mean . . . ?

B   Yes, when I'm in the middle of it? If I'm on the toilet and it's a big one and I'm squeezing it out, like it's the size of an aubergine or something?

A   Oh, I love aubergine.

B   As fat as an aubergine, yes, and it's like it gives me a hard-on?

A   But not an actual hard-on.

B   No, an actual hard-on, an actual hard-on, Louise.

A   Oh . . .

B   Yes, I know and I'm not even gay.

D   We don't have sex any more.

C   We stopped having sex after . . . you know?

B   We have sex all the time actually. She's pretty fucking wild.

A   I am wild, yes. That's just the way God made me, I'm afraid.

B   You see what I mean?

A   And I'm pretty good at it too, as a matter of fact. I'm a pretty good fuck, that is. It's all about the muscle control.

B   The muscles in her pussy. The way she contracts her muscles just as at the moment I'm about to cum?

A   And, yes, if I'm tired or if I'm bored of him or whatever. — Christ, I probably shouldn't . . .

B   Oh, don't worry, say what you like, you can . . .

C   You can say anything, Bryan. I'm not here to judge you.

D   Well, we were fairly intimate.

C   Okay. Okay, well that's good. That must have been . . . ?

D   Yes, it was actually easier than I thought. Admittedly I was drunk and . . . well, I guess I'm not that particularly well-endowed, so . . . you know?

C   Less friction.

D   Yes, the . . . friction, yes, it just . . . it just sort of slipped right in.

C   And he didn't bite?

D   No, of course he didn't bite, he's a spaniel. Spaniels don't bite.

C   Oh, sorry. Sorry, no, I'm not really . . . .

D   Yes, he was just curled up in the basket. It was gone midnight and I'd come downstairs to make a cheese sandwich and I realised . . . I'd remembered that I hadn't, I'd forgotten to take him out that day and he just looked so . . .

C   Eager?

D   Fragile, I suppose. You see I felt . . . just awful looking into those big brown eyes . . .

B   He'd forgotten to take me out that day, it was kind of a . . .

A   Problem between you?

B   No, more a mutual understanding that we bypassed with tummy strokes and leftovers or whatever. But, to be honest, I'd seen it coming for a while, so, no, my first instinct wasn't to bite. I whimpered a little maybe, but . . . but I think he gets off on that. And I was pleasantly surprised how tender he was generally. He's an incredibly sensitive human, and he doesn't bully you into immediate reciprocation like some others I could mention.

A   So you've had lots of lovers then?

B   Oh, you know. Staffs and Rottweilers mainly. The park's just full of them round here.

A   Yes, I noticed.

B   Yes, and you couldn't accuse them of being needy. I'll give them that. It's the quiet ones you've got to look out for. I mean, that Labrador next door's a total bitch.

D   Don't let him call you that again, do you promise?

C   Yes . . . no, of course.

D   That's not a very nice word for someone your age.

C   I'm going to be thirteen in June.

B   You mean you're actually twelve.

C   Well, sort of . . . Yes, I . . .

B   Eleven?

C   Eleven and three months.

B   Well you could look younger. I could make you look . . .

C   I'm actually quite cold I think, Eddie. Can I put my top back on again now?

B   Just one more for the album first. Would you hold your arms up above your head this time?

C   What, like this, you mean?

B   Exactly like that.

C   It's very quiet in here, isn't it, Eddie? Eddie . . .

A   Hey, so where is everyone? Why's it so quiet out there? Oh, so maybe you've maybe had a few drinks and you're feeling horny? Well, my name's Camilla and this is our hot new babe Lucinda and we are going to get naughty, we are going to get naked, everything for you boys. So why not dial the digits below and choose option number one and hopefully we'll be . . .

C   Hopefully we'll make it before the shops close. Hold my hand, come on.

A   I feel awkward.

C   Oh, so you do care what people think.

A   No, not . . . Don't be silly.

C   Let them think, Rachel. We're not living in Saudi for Christ'sake, hold my hand.

A   You're acting like a man.

C   What?

A   You're acting like a boyfriend, stop it.

C   Between my legs you acted like a man.

B   Everyone's getting married. I feel like I'm not allowed to be queer any more.

C   You'll feel different when you're married.

A   And it isn't true what they say about black men. That's another fucking myth.

B   Yours is smaller than mine.

D   Oh, fuck off, you haven't even measured it yet, get the ruler.

C   Excuse me?

D   Get the ruler, Sue, the ruler, it's in the top drawer.

C   I can only see a protractor!

D   Well, that'll have to do then.

A   Is it just me or are my tits getting bigger?

B   Erm . . .

C   He won't touch me unless I'm shaved. I tried growing out my Brazilian once, but he just couldn't get it up.

B   I don't like the look of them. Vaginas, I mean, sorry, it's nothing personal.

A   No, don't be sorry.

C   They're ridiculous.

A   They're delicious.

C   It just hangs there like something in a butcher's shop window.

A   I just sometimes have this urge to suck him off.

C   To suck off who off, sorry?

A   Anyone who happens to be with me, it's just this overwhelming desire . . .

B   Overwhelming desire to squeeze my thing between her tits. Up and down, the good stuff foaming over her nipples.

A   Clutching on to it with both hands, like a pole. Fuck . . .

C   Exactly like a pole, yes, and if you lick the underside.

D   Flicking her bead with the end of my tongue, and when she cums . . .

A   And my other hand, my free hand? Scratching my finger round the edge of his hole.

B   And pull the back of her skirt up when she's on that escalator in front of me.

D   To stick it in.

A   Feel it inside me. Feel him opening me up.

C   It's not true that size doesn't matter. Size does matter.

A   That feeling when we cum together and we're just looking into each other's eyes.

C   I don't think I could actually reach orgasm if it's not at least . . .

A   A baby's arm.

C   As big as a baby's arm, you're right.

B   And that top she wears with just the sides of her tits showing?

D   Side-boob, yeah, she does it on purpose.

B   Of course she fucking does it on purpose.

D   She loves it. The attention.

B   Right, and I'm on fucking fire. Makes you just want to grab hold of them and . . . and to just squeeze and bite and pull them out in front of everyone.

D   Little tits are good too.

B   Oh, little tits are excellent, perfect.

D   And did she spit or swallow?

B   Swallow.

D   Mine spits.

B   I wish Caroline would spit.

D   We keep a mug by the side of the bed.

C   Seventy-eight years old and we're still at it, aren't we, David?

B   That's right, Helen, we are.

A   And I can't look at him, he looks so stupid, so . . . serious. And with his big goofy teeth.

D   You're thinking about Ryan Gosling again aren't you?

A   I'm thinking about you, I only ever think about you.

D   She says that, but I'm actually thinking of her best friend.

B   And I've never actually done anal. Don't say it, I know that's like . . . da-dah from a gay man.

D   It is weird.

B   If he hasn't wiped properly, ugh.

D   Rimming.

B   What, sorry?

D   Rimming.

B   Oh, so you don't mind the taste of shit.

D   Well, I love the taste of his shit. In moderation of course.

C   I urinated on my fiancé during our honeymoon. Technically, he's my husband.

A   And there was one in mouth, one up my cunt, and one up my arse.

B   Our dicks actually touched didn't they, John?

D   They did, Malcolm, yes.

B   Sorry, I just thought we made quite a good team. It was quite funny, I mean.

A   Best sex I've ever had, to be honest. We've never spoken about it since.

C   Yes, and I know most people don't want to hear it, but I was turned on when he hit me.

D   She's on her knees and I'm rock fucking hard, and I just whack it across her cheek.

A   The Big Bang.

C   What?

A   The Big Bang, the . . . Oh fuck off, Lorna, you know what I'm talking about.

C   I think you've had a bit too much ouzo, don't you?

A   Look, it's all about synthesis or something f'fucksake. Sex . . . sex is just the microcosm of the universal fucking dance of life or whatever you want to . . .

C   Do you want another top-up?

A   Yes, go on then, you moron. – Christ, it's like talking to a moron.

C   The Big Bang.

A   The Big Bang, Lorna, yes. You either fuck or get eaten. You either fuck or get eaten.

C   Yes, I heard you the first time. Have another drink f'fucksake.

A   And the trouble is I don't even want children anyway.

D   My life has no meaning outside of the kids.

B   I caught them in the bedroom. I'd been dreaming about what I was going to get for my birthday and my dad just shouts at me and tells me to fuck off back to my room. I thought he was trying to murder her. I thought he was going to come for me next.

C   You dirty piece of shit. You dirty old fucker.

B   Oh, yes . . . Yes, you're right, I am! I am a piece of shit!

C   Who's been a bad boy then, eh? It's the gas chamber for you.

B   Oh God . . .

C   It's Savile's dressing room for you.

D   I actually would like to pay for it once, I think. Just to . . . you know?

C   Lindsay Lohan.

A   Who?

C   Lindsay Lohan.

D   That one from the council estate round the back. She's so needy in her tracksuit.

B   You can see her panty line.

D   Yes, her Primark fucking panty line. Her cheap little thong she wears. Sanskrit tattooed on her naval.

C   Lindsay Lohan's a bloody good actress.

A   A fireman. A pilot or something.

B   Oh, please, that's such a cliché.

C   One of my students.

B   My wife.

A   Your wife's not coming back, Neil.

D   Yes, and she's probably fucking his piggy little eyes out while we speak.

B   My wife because, believe me, the more you go through together, the better, more meaningful the sex is.

C   I mean, why is everyone so hung up about it anyway? It really shouldn't be so . . .

D   I haven't slept with anyone since the papers went through. I'm not actually . . . I don't think I'm ready.

A   He makes me laugh. We make each other laugh.

B   I'm going to go home tonight. Eat. Read a book for a bit. Have a wank. Watch TV for a bit. Have a wank, fall asleep. Wake up about seven. Have a wank, have a shower, have a wank. Lay down for a bit, get dressed. Breakfast, toilet, wank. Leave the house, get the train, go to work. Meeting at ten, fag break, wank.

A   Look, I'm telling you, if you just put a bit a coke on the end of your knob . . .

B   Under or over the foreskin?

A   My last boyfriend didn't have a foreskin. – Come on, let me dab a bit on for you, here. I promise it'll last for hours.

C   He rolls over, farts, and goes to sleep.

D   This is my first time actually.

C   Oh, get on with it then, if you must.

D   Will I wake up a different person? Because I really want to be a different person.

A   What's your favourite position?

B   Erm . . .

D   I must be the luckiest guy in the world.

C   That's because you're hot.

D   Oh, man . . .

A   How's this? Do you like this then, huh?

D   Oh man oh man oh man . . .

C   Hey, are you two going to be long? The battery's about to die on this thing.

B   And did I ever tell you were conceived on the night we saw the Rolling Stones?

D   That's pretty special, Dad.

B   It is pretty special, you're right. We slipped off to the portaloos in the middle of 'Jumping Jack Flash'.

C   Well, I know I should feel different, but to be honest . . . It was just so ordinary. If anything, I thought I was going to cry, and I just felt . . . so angry with everyone. That level of expectation, I suppose it was never going to . . .

A   I was playing in the tree with my friends. We had this beech tree at the bottom of our garden? I'd sort of watched it grow since I was a baby, and . . . and it was just part of our family, you know? Not that I'm a sentimental sort of person or anything like . . . But it was my thirteenth birthday I think, and we were playing cats and dogs, my brothers and I, and I was the cat. I was always the cat and they were being particularly vicious what with it being my birthday and everything. They're stood at the foot of the tree and they're barking and growling or whatever, and I'm climbing up as far as I can, and . . . and kind of taking the piss out of the three of them, you know? I'd been stuffing my face with chocolates and cake and all that, so I was feeling especially confident and I don't think I'd ever climbed as high as this before, and . . . And so when I slipped I was kind of . . . really fucking mortified, you know? In the split second, I mean. In the split second as I fell, and I sort of saw them all . . . my brothers, I mean. I saw them spread out, give way, and then because my dad had been trimming back the branches just the week before . . . It's like the floor was covered with old branches and there was this one particularly knotty branch and . . . Well, when I finally recovered and saw that it hadn't just broken my fall, but had actually torn a hole through my knickers. And I look down and there's blood, just . . . Running down my skinny little legs and that it wasn't ordinary blood either. Like I'd hardly a scratch on me, but I felt . . . I felt kind of woozy, and I suddenly had this overwhelming need to pee, with my brothers just staring at me in horror and disgust. . . . Anyway, I think someone must have carried me inside, and my mother runs me a bath. And about a day or two later, my dad comes back home with this fucking chainsaw and that was the end of the tree.

C   It's not that I'm scared of it or anything. It's just one of many choices that one must make if you are to devote your life to God. Yes. Yes, and I know that some people would find that —

B   Christ, those lips, look.

C   — unusual, and I'd never lie and say that I've never felt certain physical urges.

A   I can't remember, did Jesus actually fuck Mary Magdalene or what?

D   Well, we know that the Queen shagged Prince Philip.

C   More than once.

D   More than once, I know!

B   Team meeting that goes on all afternoon. Have a shit, have a wank. Talk to Julie from accounts, think about having a wank. Work on the budget, get distracted . . .

A   Have a wank, go to sleep. Work through Thursday, get to Friday. The work do's cancelled, so go home. Watch a bit of telly, eat my salad, have a wank. Feel disgusted with myself, have a wank. Wait for Peter to get home.

C   He won't latch on, I keep telling you f'Christ's sake, it's not that I'm not trying!

D   The missus swallowed after a blow job for the first time in five years last night . . . I wonder if it's a sign she's coming out of her coma?

B   What's the difference between oral sex and anal sex?

D   Oral sex makes your day; anal sex makes your hole weak.

B   What do a gynaecologist and a pizza delivery boy have in common?

D   They can both smell it but can't eat it.

B   How is a woman like a condom?

D   Both spend more time in your wallet than on your dick.

B   What is the similarity between a woman and KFC?

D   By the time you've finished with the breasts and thighs, all you have left is a greasy box to put your bone in.

B   Jack and Jill went up the hill
So Jack could lick Jill's fanny
Jack got a shock and a mouthful of cock
'Cause Jill's a pre-op tranny!

D   Mary had a little snatch,
A teeny-tiny hole,
Johnny couldn't quite fit in,
His massive manly pole.
He greased her up and squirmed and shoved,
And pinched her little tit,
But nothing seemed to work for him,
The damned thing wouldn't fit!
So Mary drank a lot of wine,
And smoked a little grass,
And just as she was passing out,
He shoved it up her . . .

C   What's the difference between a G-spot and a golf ball?

A   A man will spend twenty minutes looking for a golf ball.

C   What have men and floor tiles got in common?

A   If you lay them properly, you can walk on them for the rest of your life!

A   What is the insensitive bit at the base of the penis called?

C   The man.

A   Ahh, it's cute. Who circumcised you?

C   Why don't we just cuddle?

A   Wow, and your feet are so big.

C   It's okay, we'll work around it.

A   Will it squeak if I squeeze it?

C   Look, can I be honest with you?

A   Were you neutered?

C   I don't actually think this is going to work.

B   I know, so do I. I feel . . . I feel . . .

A   I like feel closer to you somehow?

B   Yeah, I know, like . . . Weird though, isn't it?

A   It is weird, yeah. Good though.

C   And will you be calling him again?

A   I'll see him at school, won't I?

C   Look, I know what you were doing up there.

A   We were doing our homework, Mum, we've got our SATs in a week. Oh, leave off . . .

D   You're fucking filthy, you know that?

A   Yeah, well, if you'd get on with it a second instead of giving me a running commentary half the time.

D   Yeah, well, your mum's going to go mental isn't she? The state of these sheets already.

A   Oh, fuck off, Mark, 'the sheets'. She can fuck off out my life for once.

D   Is that the right hole?

A   That's my arsehole, you div, don't be so polite all the time. 'Ere, come on, let me give me you a hand again f'Christ's sake. It's wet and in the middle there, look.

B   I'm afraid the results have come back positive.

A   You mean like . . . ?

C   Don't worry it's easily cured. Your father and I . . .

B   Gonorrhoea, herpes – they're all relatively . . .

D To be honest, my sex life has improved since I was diagnosed. If there's anything HIV has taught me, it's to make me realise the virtue of monogamy. I used to be so hung up about getting close to another man. Of real intimacy, you know? And now that we're both positive, it's given us a real chance to build a life together. That is until of course one of us . . .

C I'm not sure he can hear us.

B He's gone.

Long pause.

C I think we should say a prayer.

Pause.

Wouldn't you rather say a prayer now, do you think?

Pause.

He'll be safer now in Heaven.

A Do you think they fuck in Heaven?

B What, all those little angels with their miniature pricks?

C They should take him away, I can't stand it. They should get his body out of here before it . . .

B Yes, and it's all done with the utmost care, you understand? We don't just dispose of the body like it's some sort of . . .

D Like meat.

B It's important we have full access to the patient's . . .

D The deceased's.

B To the deceased's body while we . . .

D All his major organs in fact.

B Yes, while we perform the autopsy.

D   Which is just a matter of routine. There's no need to be alarmed, it's all done . . .

B   Like I say, it's all done with the utmost care. And in fact, interestingly, the trickiest bit is removing the tongue and windpipe.

D   What we'll do is we'll put the body on the slab and we'll cut . . .

B   We cut, we loosen.

D   We work up under the skin from the chest. Then the skin around the jawline is loosened, and then we'll work the blade to slice around the tongue. Both that and the windpipe can then be pulled out from under the jaw.

B   And once we've removed all the organs, they're then taken to the bench and we'll go through them one by one to check their weight and look for blocked vessels and so forth.

D   And we slice through the lungs to see if there if there are any tumours.

B   Naturally, it's important we work quickly so that the flies don't have a chance to settle in.

D   Before the body starts to liquefy.

B   To putrify, yes. In a couple of days, that is.

D   Yes, and of course it can be alarming to see what was once a healthy human body . . .

B   Big tits and little tits.

D   Big cocks and little cocks. Yes, to see them all . . .

B   To see them this way.

D   And, of course, with all the blood and bile that you'd imagine. I mean, we're literally soaked.

B   Sorry, you must be . . .

D   Yes, you must be, yes, sorry.

B I mean, it is quite a leveller I suppose. Did you know that there are about eight billion people living on the planet today? I mean, that's . . .

D That's a lot of bodies.

B That's a lot of sex.

A Dreams, you mean?

C Fantasies.

A Sexually, I mean. Not that I'm frigid.

C I'm not sure that I've met anyone who could live up to my fantasies of what . . .

D Of what they're thinking out there.

B Yes, out there, just . . . staring through here, look. It's important we get the sight-lines.

D So, she should be standing about here you think? Say, about here?

C I think she should she be sitting rather than standing.

B Sitting definitely. Lounging in fact. They can get a better look at her tits that way, look.

D Yes, but it's rather unnatural isn't it?

B She's the most natural thing on the planet, look. She's perfect. You're perfect aren't you, sweetheart?

A Yes, I suppose so.

B Tell me, they are natural, aren't they?

A Oh, natural as in . . . ?

D Well, my penis is a 100 per cent natural.

A Completely, yes, there's no way I could ever afford . . .

B Well, they feel natural to me. Do they feel natural to you?

C   Oh, yes, lovely. Lovely yes, juicy. Juicy.

A   You make the most of what you've got.

B   What you've got, yes. You know it's times like this when I just feel like . . .

C   Yes, I know what you mean. Do you think you could help me with my bra strap?

B   I mean, we're all adults here, aren't we? There's nothing to be ashamed of.

D   (*showing his cock*)   Hey, look everyone!

The chorus of Prince's 'Get Off'. **A**, **B**, **C** *and* **D** *move to the music.*

The music ends, then . . .

B   Today is a good day for penetration. The sun's out, it's a bank holiday.

D   No, I'm fucked, I couldn't.

A   I want another one.

B   What, already? But we've only just had . . .

A   I want another one, David, please.

C   Look, she can make up her own mind, alright? These things happen, it's natural.

A   It's the most natural thing in the world.

B   Those fucking lips, and those big round fuck-me eyes.

A   Play with my nipples while he's falling asleep in front of the football downstairs. Have a wank.

D   Oh, look, he's started, look.

C   What?

D   He's latched on, he's . . .

C   Oh God, yes. So he has. He's actually . . .

D   Daddy's little boy.

C   Well, he's actually hurting me a bit.

B   Those eyes, that body — Christ, I'd fuck her. I really would fuck her.

A   Stop it, you're hurting me.

B   I'd fuck her like this. Like this.

A   You're hurting my feelings, Philip, stop it!

D   But if you don't know how I feel . . .

A   You've told me again and again how you feel. Look, can't we just . . . ?

D   All my life my head tells me one thing and my heart tells me another.

B   Your cock, you mean.

D   Hm?

B   Your cock. It tells you one thing . . .

C   You know I started quite young really. Ironically, it was only a few months after my hysterectomy, but . . . you know? Actually I'm relieved.
For a long time I tried to convince, to will myself that I was still somehow . . .
Attracted or available, or that I even felt the urge any more.
I'd sit and cry and punish myself and think that my own body had betrayed me and that surely there must some small part of me that still needed to be . . . in that way, and that without it I was less of a woman or that I wasn't a woman at all.
Three times a week, once a week.

Once a fortnight, a month, once every six months, a year.
I don't miss it.
I prefer it. That restless itch always.
Like a kid again.
Like a . . . little kid at Christmas.
I'm a much better person I think.

Do It!

Do It! was recorded as part of the Royal Court's Open Court season and was first broadcast at the Royal Court Theatre, London, on 12 June 2013, with the following cast and creative team:

Man   Alan Williams
Voices   Doon Mackichan
                 Selene Hizli
                 Natasha Gordon
                 Al Weaver

Director Ned Bennett
Producer Carissa Hope Lynch

Characters

Man
Voice One
Voice Two
Voice Three
Voice Four

White noise, collapsing/colliding radio signals, until the voice of
a **Man** *emerges.*

Man   Okay, it's that one . . .
That one there, right there . . . In the suit, the blue suit . . . Do you
see him? I asked you a question, do you see him?
Piece of shit, you're not looking properly, in the suit. The blue,
the dark blue suit, keep your eyes on him, don't . . . Keep your
eyes on him, where's he going?
Who's he talking to, where?
Where's he going, you've lost him, haven't you?
Give me the signal, is he still in range?

You've lost him, haven't you?
Give me the signal.
Give me the signal, cunt, don't stand there.
Don't just stand there, don't . . . Turn the fuck around!

Can you hear me?

Okay.
Raise your hand if you can hear me.
Raise your right hand, raise your hand.
Raise your right hand. – Alright, don't make it obvious, just . . .
Just raise your hand a little bit. Put it on the ledge, the balcony.
Raise your right hand and rest it on the balcony.
Have you done it?
On the balcony, the ledge because I can see you, we can all . . .
We can all see you and that man in the blue suit over there.

Alright, who else? Who else do you see?
Which else of these bastards?
What, that disgusting rich bitch with her shopping bags?
That other rich bitch with her husband or whatever he thinks he is.
The kids? Oh, you're cold. You're a cold fucking bastard, aren't
you?

Have you made your choice?

Raise your finger, have you made your choice?

The choice is yours.

Do it.

Do it.

Do it.

Do it.

Do it.

Do it.

Do it now.

Do it.

Do it.

Do it.

Do it.

Do it. – What, are you totally incompetent? You have to make a –

White noise, collapsing/colliding radio signals, until . . .

Voice One   – sense of everything, anything, in just my everyday day-to-day life and try to balance and to put my house in order. As they say, and that I'm . . .

Voice Two   Weighed down without even trying, and I'm putting on this thing, this face and with everyone pulling at it, and without even meaning to, right? Trying to pull at this face I've worked my whole fucking life to master, to perfect and to put it out there . . . Put it out there, my face, my whole fucking –

Voice One   'Hello, it's me again' and so everyone can see that it is me, everyone knows it is me because they recognise my face and you say . . . You and I both say all the right things because you've spent what feels like a lifetime perfecting and working out –

Voice Two   My imperfections to a tee because I don't want to seem –

Voice Three   I don't want to appear anything other than neutral. I don't want to seem in any way that I'm above, or that people can't reach me if they want to, that I'm open, a good open book, a classic, a Penguin classic —

Voice Two   Human and stupid and selfish and wrong some of the time and, and yet right some of the time.

Voice Three   Ready to listen, always ready to see the other side of the story and . . . without prejudice, with some openness objectivity reason. And fuck off, no, I'm not Mahatma Gandhi, I'm not. Fickle and contrary . . .

Voice Four   The rest of us I should say, an essential roundabout human.

Voice One   Not that I'd ever want to be a saint — who wants that?

Voice Three   I mean, if someone or something comes along and for once I have to be a bit fucking . . . yes, a bit fucking ruthless from time to time. Sometimes you have to say no when it counts and even lose your temper or say the wrong thing —

Voice Two   Maybe tweet something that might lose me a few friends, fuck it.

Voice One   I don't actually need any of these people.

Voice Four   Accounted and accountable for my actions, and in no way taking the moral high ground, I can't stand that. I can't stand people who take the moral high ground.

Voice Two   And I do know people who do do that.

Voice Three   And here, right now, today, in a democracy. The same whatever, the same weight that's pressing down on you, testing your limits as a compassionate human being.

Voice One   Make the best of what you've got. Work. Give time and space and patience to your friends and family. And some people don't see the world in the same way, that's fine

Voice Two   That's perfectly fine. Ultimately . . .

Voice Three   To endeavour for ourselves, for our own fucking selves.

Voice Four   I'm immune to criticism, I have to be. I know I'm capable of being selfish, I know there are far better ways to spend my time. Productive, positive . . .

Voice Two   Because I like to treat myself like anyone else does.

Voice Four   And if there are other people, other cultures who can't or won't, or who don't have the same . . .

Voice Three   Live in the here and now, in the most democratic way possible, that's my right. And yes, I work and I . . .

Voice One   Try my hardest to give you space, because I really do think we could get along and I'm a nice person. I'm a good person actually, and the people around me, my friends – my friends and my family – they think so.

Voice Four   Quite a good, interesting, funny, fun person to be around –

Voice Two   Neutral.

Voice One   Because I'm someone who listens, and someone who isn't afraid of admitting when they're wrong.

Voice Two   Look good, feel good, to look and feel my best.

Voice Three   Project some degree of civilised, moral behaviour. Knowing all the time I shit and piss like anyone else, this thing, this animal.

Voice Two   Just shit and eat and –

Voice One   Eat and shit each other out.

Voice Four   Even the most persuasive kind of person can't . . .

Voice Three   Feel good when you give to charity.

Voice Two   To feel better than you do anyway, and I swear to God I would never exchange my life for yours or hers or him over there.

Voice Four   For me, my life has to be better than yours, it just has to be, sorry. I mean, who the hell else is . . . ?

Voice Three   A sort of necessary suffering.

Voice Two   Make eye-contact or not. Just try to . . .

Voice Three   Accommodate everyone else's bullshit, and that I couldn't give a fuck about, and then I feel guilty, and feel better for feeling guilty.

Voice One   Lay awake at night, going round and round in circles . . .

Voice Four   And that you might even be attracted to me a little bit.

Voice Three   Just some, I don't know, respect.

Voice Two   At least because, essentially, I'm just an easy-going, nice friendly day-to-day sort of . . .

White noise, colliding/collapsing radio signals, until the voice of the **Man** *emerges.*

Man   Okay, it's that one . . .
That one there, right there . . . In the suit, the blue suit . . . Do you see him? I asked you a question, do you see him?
Piece of shit, you're not looking properly, in the suit. The blue, the dark-blue suit, keep your eyes on him, don't . . . Keep your eyes on him, where's he going?
Who's he talking to, where?
Where's he going, you've lost him, haven't you?
Give me the signal, is he still in range?

And repeat.

Bloomsbury Methuen Drama Contemporary Dramatists

include

John Arden (two volumes)
Arden & D'Arcy
Peter Barnes (three volumes)
Sebastian Barry
Mike Bartlett
Dermot Bolger
Edward Bond (eight volumes)
Howard Brenton (two volumes)
Leo Butler
Richard Cameron
Jim Cartwright
Caryl Churchill (two volumes)
Complicite
Sarah Daniels (two volumes)
Nick Darke
David Edgar (three volumes)
David Eldridge (two volumes)
Ben Elton
Per Olov Enquist
Dario Fo (two volumes)
Michael Frayn (four volumes)
John Godber (four volumes)
Paul Godfrey
James Graham
David Greig
John Guare
Lee Hall (two volumes)
Katori Hall
Peter Handke
Jonathan Harvey (two volumes)
Iain Heggie
Israel Horovitz
Declan Hughes
Terry Johnson (three volumes)
Sarah Kane
Barrie Keeffe
Bernard-Marie Koltès (two volumes)
Franz Xaver Kroetz
Kwame Kwei-Armah
David Lan
Bryony Lavery
Deborah Levy
Doug Lucie

David Mamet (four volumes)
Patrick Marber
Martin McDonagh
Duncan McLean
David Mercer (two volumes)
Anthony Minghella (two volumes)
Tom Murphy (six volumes)
Phyllis Nagy
Anthony Neilson (two volumes)
Peter Nichol (two volumes)
Philip Osment
Gary Owen
Louise Page
Stewart Parker (two volumes)
Joe Penhall (two volumes)
Stephen Poliakoff (three volumes)
David Rabe (two volumes)
Mark Ravenhill (three volumes)
Christina Reid
Philip Ridley (two volumes)
Willy Russell
Eric-Emmanuel Schmitt
Ntozake Shange
Sam Shepard (two volumes)
Martin Sherman (two volumes)
Christopher Shinn
Joshua Sobel
Wole Soyinka (two volumes)
Simon Stephens (three volumes)
Shelagh Stephenson
David Storey (three volumes)
C. P. Taylor
Sue Townsend
Judy Upton
Michel Vinaver (two volumes)
Arnold Wesker (two volumes)
Peter Whelan
Michael Wilcox
Roy Williams (four volumes)
David Williamson
Snoo Wilson (two volumes)
David Wood (two volumes)
Victoria Wood

Bloomsbury Methuen Drama Modern Plays

include work by

Bola Agbaje
Edward Albee
Davey Anderson
Jean Anouilh
John Arden
Peter Barnes
Sebastian Barry
Alistair Beaton
Brendan Behan
Edward Bond
William Boyd
Bertolt Brecht
Howard Brenton
Amelia Bullmore
Anthony Burgess
Leo Butler
Jim Cartwright
Lolita Chakrabarti
Caryl Churchill
Lucinda Coxon
Curious Directive
Nick Darke
Shelagh Delaney
Ishy Din
Claire Dowie
David Edgar
David Eldridge
Dario Fo
Michael Frayn
John Godber
Paul Godfrey
James Graham
David Greig
John Guare
Mark Haddon
Peter Handke
David Harrower
Jonathan Harvey
Iain Heggie

Robert Holman
Caroline Horton
Terry Johnson
Sarah Kane
Barrie Keeffe
Doug Lucie
Anders Lustgarten
David Mamet
Patrick Marber
Martin McDonagh
Arthur Miller
D. C. Moore
Tom Murphy
Phyllis Nagy
Anthony Neilson
Peter Nichols
Joe Orton
Joe Penhall
Luigi Pirandello
Stephen Poliakoff
Lucy Prebble
Peter Quilter
Mark Ravenhill
Philip Ridley
Willy Russell
Jean-Paul Sartre
Sam Shepard
Martin Sherman
Wole Soyinka
Simon Stephens
Peter Straughan
Kate Tempest
Theatre Workshop
Judy Upton
Timberlake Wertenbaker
Roy Williams
Snoo Wilson
Frances Ya-Chu Cowhig
Benjamin Zephaniah

For a complete listing of Bloomsbury
Methuen Drama titles, visit:

www.bloomsbury.com/drama

Follow us on Twitter and keep up to date
with our news and publications

@MethuenDrama

CPSIA information can be obtained
at www.ICGtesting.com
Printed in the USA
FFOW01n2033200416
23405FF